Holy Spirit
My Coach

HOLY SPIRIT MY COACH

Harrison S. Mungal

Copyright © 2008 by Harrison S. Mungal.

ISBN:	Softcover	978-1-4363-6310-5

PRINTED 2008

All rights reserved. This book is protected under the copyright laws of Canada. This book may not be copied or reprinted for commercial gain or profit. The use of short quotation or occasional page copying for personal or group study is permitted and encouraged. Permission will be granted upon request. Unless otherwise identified, Scripture quotations are from The New King James Version of the Bible.

This book was printed in the United States of America.

For Worldwide Distribution.

First Edition

To order additional copies of this book, contact:
Xlibris Corporation
1-888-795-4274
www.Xlibris.com
Orders@Xlibris.com
43196

Contents

Introduction	9
"I Am He"	11
My First Encounter	17
Gods	21
My Healing	25
Power	29
All Hail the Power . . .	37
Receiving the Promise	41
Baptism	45
My First Sermon	51
Walk with Me	57
My Coach	59
The Right Setting	61
Dependency	63
Dispel this Fear	67
Gifts	69
Fruit	73
Wind	75
Fire	77
Friendship	81
Signs and Symbols	85
Freedom	89
Forever with Him	95
Savour the Fragrance	99
Preparation	103
Anointing	107
Our Position	115
The Vision	121

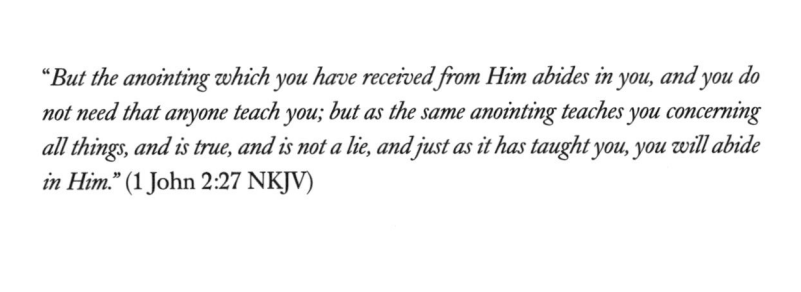

"But the anointing which you have received from Him abides in you, and you do not need that anyone teach you; but as the same anointing teaches you concerning all things, and is true, and is not a lie, and just as it has taught you, you will abide in Him." (1 John 2:27 NKJV)

INTRODUCTION

AFTER MY ENCOUNTER with the Holy Spirit that one Sunday morning, that was quite unexpected, the power of God came down upon me. It was another confirmation of His realness. During this occurrence I felt the exhilaration of electricity flowing through my whole body. This incident was accompanied by the thrill of releasing my stumbling tongue into the music of that heavenly language for which I so ardently sought. When it did happen I was unprepared for the smooth flow coming forth from deep within. This brought about a transformation within, my hunger was satisfied and my thirst was quenched and I felt the fulfilment of this intense need being met beyond my human expectation. It was just what I needed to confirm my quest to know the Holy Spirit. This experience pushed me into the next step of wanting to be coached by the Holy Spirit.

Ever since that first encounter with the Holy Spirit my life has never been the same. Working with the Holy Spirit has brought maturity and broadened my horizon to explore the plan, purpose and destiny God designed for my life. He has developed a passion in me to appreciate the lives of others. I see humanity has one ultimate purpose for living and that is to enjoy the benefits of all God has prepared for those who love Him. Each day with the Holy Spirit is an adventure full of excitement and surprises as He leads into breaking new grounds. His main goal is to help reach our full potential.

The book will take you into another dimension of maturity with the Holy Spirit. You will develop a liking to spend quality time with the person of the Holy Spirit, as He becomes your coach and you become addicted to His presence. You will explore new horizons and experience the joy of being a Christian. As He breathes upon you and fills you with the power and strength needed for each birthing experience, you will never be the same again. He will coach you all the way into birthing new visions and dreams destined by God for your life.

You will learn about the person of the Holy Spirit, His role and responsibility and our ability to work with Him. You will circumnavigate all the necessities that will draw you closer to Him. He will become the fragrance of your being and your world will recognize a greater energy force behind your walk in life.

This book is dedicated to my parents, especially my dad for encouraging me to explore the reality of God, and to pursue truth.

"I AM HE"

The Birth Of Our Second Child, the birthdate is April 12 instead of April 23.

MY DAY BEGAN at 02:00hrs on weekdays with earnest prayers. This was the time I allocated to enter my prayer closet to worship the Lord and fellowship with the Holy Spirit. It was during this time of dedication that something wonderful and incredible took place which brought about a glorious change in my life.

It had been over six months, since my quest to be in full communion with the Holy Spirit. It was a time in my life where I hungered to feel the presence of the Lord, as I did when I was first saved. I spent many early mornings at a secluded place next to the Welland Canal in St. Catherines, Ontario. At dawn I would drive to the canal, where I would spend hours in prayer. Sometimes it was very cold that when the temperature dropped it was almost unbearable. Despite this obstacle I kept my appointment, I knew that I needed a closer relationship with the Holy Spirit. He was all I had, and it was only Him who understood me.

This was a time in my life when I realized how much I needed Him. My wife was expecting our second child; I was in Bible College, attending classes from 07:00 a.m. until 12:00 noon, and I worked from 13:00-21:30 hours. I did not have the luxury of spending much time with my family, and I realized that time was a scarce commodity. I realized my need to be nurtured spiritually before I could develop into the person God was preparing to use. Many spiritual men recognized the call upon my life, yet I received no offer of mentorship from these spiritual giants. I was like 'a Timothy' but there was 'no Paul' for me. No one was willing to take me under their wing to guide me.

My task therefore was to find my way in the world with the Holy Spirit as my guide. As I submitted under leadership from whom I could learn, I found myself being used as a stepping stool for their personal gain. I was disappointed on several occasions yet I strove to study in spite of the obstacles that came my way. There were other challenges in my personal life also that were overwhelming; I was a young father with little financial resources and the responsibility of a growing family. Yet I was determined to submit and pursue my call, and with the help of the Lord I persisted in equipping myself with the necessary tools needed for this pilgrimage. My faith and the love of God was the driving force, while persistency and consistency were the key elements in my dedication to fulfil my destiny. I realized my call would not materialize without some sacrifice as failure to study and commit could only result in my being a spiritual dwarf. I told myself that there is never a better time to prepare like now. If I wait on the opportune time it may never come, and I will only live a life of failure and regrets.

I learnt at an early age that fellowshipping with the Holy Spirit should be my first step. The early morning meetings in prayer gave me strength in my purpose and praying by the canal brought peace and tranquillity. I recall my first encounter with the Holy Spirit; words are inadequate to express the joy and peace that came over me when I experienced being filled with His power. It was during this fellowship with Him that the vision for the ministry became crystal clear. I had launched out in ministry just a year before and it was the relationship I had developed with the Holy Spirit that kept me moving forward. As I got involved in my personal responsibilities and commitment I found myself drifting away from my former love, not spending enough time with Him in prayer as I used to do in the past.

Early one morning while I was at the canal, there the wind was blowing and I felt a power in the wind. In that moment a thought flashed across my mind – This is how I should experience the Holy Spirit. Then suddenly this was no longer a thought but a journey I embarked upon. I hungered for the experience to come to fruition. During this time, my wife was already nine months pregnant with our second child. I had a delicate balance to maintain – trying to spend quality time with her was my obligation and keeping my schedule of prayer was a priority I could not avoid in any way. In fact as my responsibilities grew, the need for prayer grew. I found I needed to be coached while my wife depended on me to coach her through this pregnancy.

The Birth of Our Second Child

It was the month of April, spring was in the air and recent showers left the air brisk and clean and the ground quite wet. On Friday, April 12, 1993 at approximately 18:30 hours, my wife announced she was having labour pains. The hospital was about an hour and fifteen minutes away and I was to drive her there. In the car we checked the time lapse between each contraction and realized they were getting progressively closer at an alarming rate. Then suddenly my wife informed me that the baby was on its way and requested that we stop the vehicle. This news set me at a different pace, I did not heed my wife's appeal to stop, instead my feet applied pressure to the accelerator and I proceeded though every red traffic light driving above the speed limit in a desperate attempt to arrive at the hospital before baby's arrival. I did not stop until I reached the emergency entrance of the hospital. Upon arrival the baby was in a breach position, the legs purple and blue already outside my wife's body. My wife was ushered immediately into the delivery room. I was in the delivery room with her as the doctor assessed her situation, then he advised us that he needed extra medical support to deliver the baby. He went on to say that surgery is required because of the breached position the baby was in.

While he was out of the room looking for additional support, I laid my hands on my wife's abdomen and began to pray. I recalled saying "devil, you are a liar and this baby will be born". While praying, the baby was birthed, still in the breached position. I had to call a nurse to aid in the delivery. The doctor came back flabbergasted, and then said "this is a miracle baby". There were no complications and both my wife and our baby daughter were fine.

On my way home that night, the Holy Spirit began showing me a bigger picture of the call on my life. I was shown how much the Holy Spirit wanted to be my coach, mirroring my situation to that of my wife. I had coached her all the way through the delivery. The Holy Spirit showed me that although I was tired, I kept focused and was persistent in making sure that she was cared for properly. This night was a watershed in my life. I had a lengthy conversation with the Holy Spirit through the night, as He showed me what I needed to do in order to birth the ministry to which God called me.

One important task of being a coach in preparing for the delivery of a child was to time the contractions. Changes in the intervals, strength, and frequency of contractions are all important tips to remember. Two things I learnt were the importance of time as well as keeping a mental record of all the other associated activities. The Holy Spirit as my coach gave me the confidence. I was conscious that time is an important factor when the call of God for the ministry is ready to be birthed. Keeping a record of occurrences was essential since our human tendencies would easily dismiss these signals as coincidences, which could thwart the impending launch. Revelation through the word of God can be the announcement that by faith we are to be propelled into action, then lo and behold the ministry has been birthed, and all else is history.

The parallel of being coach to my wife became a mirrored image of the work of the Holy Spirit in my life. The birth pangs and whatever else could go wrong was in His power. He is in the driver seat and we just have to obey as the signals were received. In retrospect though the labour pains caused her much despair it was brief, and her dependence for comfort and guidance from me uplifted her spirit and gave her strength, so it is with the Holy Spirit who will stay close by our side and work with us as we become stronger in Him. We need to recognize that He is with us as our helper and supporter.

When I picture the Holy Spirit as my coach birthing the call of God in my life, I am aware that He is in full control of the situation. I realize how important it is to step out in faith at His bidding. There is never an occasion for doubt, and I can have confidence in Him as my guide. Like at childbirth we have to acquaint ourselves with the signals He gives. I have learnt that I have to surrender to His calm yet firm and confident way as He touches me, and to listen to His encouraging voice as He encourages me. His constant presence by my side was uplifting and kept me focused. Like the attending husband He uses a breathing pattern to help the birthing process. The Holy Spirit breathes upon us and fills us with the power and strength needed for each birthing experience. He breathes the breath of life. For me He whispered in a still small voice to keep me calm. He never ever gives up and keeps on coaching until the end. Like a husband, the Holy Spirit is considerate and does everything to ease the burden, He is our comforter.

The experience that night after our second baby daughter was born brought about a significant change in my life. I spent the entire night basking in the presence of the Holy Spirit. After my wife came home with the baby, the Holy Spirit kept reminding me about the spiritual baby that needed to be birthed. He showed me that I needed to do the same.

It took six months of intimacy with the Lord to bring me to this awareness. It could have been longer but God is the great planner, as for my part I was to continue with the Holy Spirit regardless and continue to make every effort to keep my commitment with Him. This incident gave me a new driving force to continue without any specific expectation. God knows my need and my desire and he will only implement situations in my life to fulfil the destiny for which he has created me. I set my alarm to wake up at 02:00am in the morning. I would retire to a spare room where I had a cassette player with worship songs. A second alarm was also in this room, so if I felt like sleeping in, because of the secondary alarm in the spare room I was forced to get up to turn it off. Once I was up I was ready to go and I would then put on the gospel tapes, while I attended to my personal needs to refresh myself and welcome the day.

Weeks went by as I continue to welcome the Holy Spirit. There were times when I had the distinct impression that someone had entered the room. Other times I felt like someone turned on the lights which were already on but the light increased its intensity. I was persistent in pursuing the intense desire to experience an encounter with the Holy Spirit. There were times when all I could do was moan and groan as though I was grieving for the lost of someone dear. I pleaded with God to release me of this passionate unrest deep within me. I was mesmerized by this magnetic yet elusive power that continued to fascinate me. It was there in the air like a lure that was so real, yet unreachable. This quest brought me closer and closer into the presence of the Lord.

I continued my unrelenting quest prayerfully when suddenly, one morning; I felt someone entered my room. My immediate response was to rebuke the spirit of fear. I heard an audible voice say, "I am He" and then the wind blew me up against the wall of my prayer room. Suddenly there was a surge of emotions, I was weeping as I felt the tangible presence of the Holy Spirit. I felt powerless before this majestic presence, as a beggar before a king. My legs became weak. I felt like a candle burning with an intense flame. I was like wax, melting before the presence of the Lord. I felt like my old skin was being replaced. The presence of the Lord was so real; and there I was in suspense. I felt like a feather, yet heavy like a rock. The entire room was filled with this awesome presence. As I lifted my hands, I felt like my body was up against silk. The atmosphere was heavy yet full of peace and joy.

That morning changed my life. I now knew what the Holy Spirit meant about being a close friend, and working with me as a coach. The message was clear that He is my Coach, and will be working with me and with Him we will achieve the gold medallion in the race before us. Like the athletes who spend quality time in training makes it to the Olympics, but unlike the world every committed soul is rewarded. The world looks on as we thrive to conquer while we endure the temptations of life. They realize our efforts are truly a sacrifice and they salute our perseverance while we offer it up back to God. My gold medallion was not in tangible gold but the assignment of another level of ministry. This is the type of reward with which the Lord remunerates us and like the athlete we feel honoured and set out to show ourselves worthy of our new goal. This was what the Lord was showing me and I reached out as I entered into another level of ministry

MY FIRST ENCOUNTER

I HAD MY first encounter with the Holy Spirit when I was about 7 years old. I wept for over three hours non-stop as He touched me. I could not explain what was happening to me. I felt like I was being made clean, like water running all over my body. My emotions were all stirred up. I saw an innocent God dying for me. I felt ashamed, knowing that someone else paid the price for my life and now I belonged to someone who cared for me. I felt the power of the cross and the innocent blood shed for me. All I knew was that the message I heard from the preacher that night did something to me internally and no one could convince me any less.

It took approximately seven years for me to make a final decision to follow Jesus and to make Him Lord of my life. I was caught up in a situation that required strength, to defy loved ones for something I cannot explain was beyond me as I grew up in an atmosphere where children obeyed their elders. I had to deal with the culture I was born into, religion and pressure from others put me under great stress. It was not until I was looking death in the face that I had to make the decision of my life. I became very ill at the age of fourteen, with an unidentified blood disorder. I was bedridden and weak, unable to help myself. My mother would answer to all my personal needs. I was shy and I felt so embarrassed when she attended to me. It was an already challenging period of my life psychologically and emotionally, but I was helpless and had to surrender to others.

I was a devout Hindu, born to Hindu parents. I was faithful to this religion and served the numerous gods diligently. I attended a Hindu elementary school, where the students were indoctrinated into the religion. Then at home my mother were very committed. I offered up prayers in the morning, mid-day and evening. Our prayers were ritualistic and repetitive, and I had it down pat. It was so ingrained in my memory that even now after over twenty years I can still recite them all. Part of the ritual was at dawn I had to offer milk to "mother earth" facing the east. I identified the god this offering was being made to by carrying a home made flag of a specific colour. As the milk was poured on the earth it was absorbed but we were led to believe that it was the gods that were drinking the milk. A tangible way of recognizing these gods were through pictures and idols made in like forms. Other forms of offering were in money and food prepared specially for them and was offered to the fire. I was dutiful to these observances. I had to be clean so I washed before prayers and dressed in white for purity. I sang with all my heart as I devoted myself in prayer.

I did have questions regarding the conviction of others that participated in these rituals as I did, who some later would become intoxicated, rapist and molesters, thieves, cheating others, and living a life of adultery. Then I realized that service to these gods were only for the moment when sacrifices were performed. They came with a need and adhered to what was expected of them. This corrupt life style raised questions in my heart. I could not see the difference of being godly, serving millions of gods, compared to those who did not have a god.

Although my parents were poor, my mother would have a ceremony, where there was food to feed the entire village. Invitations were not given, it was a public function and all were welcome. We were led to believe that feeding the poor appeased the gods. Accommodation or catering to the needs was never a problem. Attendees would squat on the floor or ground prepared for seating, a large edible leaf would suffice as a plate and they ate with their fingers. Water and a home cooked meal were provided. In fact the week prior to the religious function fruits and vegetables would be bought and stored. Only vegetarian meals were served, everyone abstained from meats during these offered prayers. For those whose could afford to serve in dishes, particular care was taken to keep the dishes separate from those in which meat is served during non-religious functions. The gods did not approve of any kind of meat because they were considered unclean; as such any dish in which meats were served in was contaminated. The cooking was simple and neighbours and friends would volunteer to help.

It was against this backdrop that the Lord called me. And so it was at 14 years of age that I recalled all that I have read and heard about Jesus. The miracles and the healings He performed, and that He could do it again. My faith soared as I called out to Him and dedicated my life to His service. I claimed that which I knew He could do and He came to my aid. This healing miracle impacted more than my life (I will explain my miraculous healing a little later in the book). Others in my immediate family who were Hindus became believers including my mother. All things connected with the Hindu religion were destroyed. Many that resisted this faith of Christianity were now willing to abandon all their beliefs for this great healer. My life was a testimony of the God I am now serving. My born again experience was something real and alive.

As I reflected on my old faith I saw that people were able to cheat, steal, become drunk, smoke while polluting their body and other worldly activities, then for a short time they would attend one of their pagan rituals and for that time they felt they were clean before their gods. The physical aspect and the abstinence or fast was all that mattered. Christianity on the other hand is a heart changing process, whether we are in church, with Christians or by ourselves, we know that God is all knowing and all seeing and all present.

I recalled being in my grandmother's home at about the age of seven. Her house was built on stilts raised about six or seven feet above the concrete foundation. The living quarters were upstairs. This was common for houses in that area. The only exception was the lavatory which was an outhouse known as a latrine. This was basically a shed built over a hole in the ground. This was how the poor lived. Only the rich had toilets in their living quarters with a septic tank outside where the refuse was accumulated. Under her house makeshift benches were constructed from very rough lumber. They were about twelve feet long and one foot wide. A wooden pulpit constructed from odds and ends was set up just big enough to house a bible. This was the setting for a Christian church.

In a village of faithful Hindu worshippers a spirit-filled church was birthed. The pastor introduced Jesus as a healer to the people. After evangelizing he started with a group of about 25 people in the humble quarters under my grandmother's house. Soon this small group grew as the power of God moved. When the Christians worshipped, it would feel like a strong wind passing through the service. People would drop to the ground; others would be dancing, and I was told they are "dancing in the spirit". I remembered vividly, that even when my eyes were closed I heard people dropping on the hard concrete floor and I was told this happened when the Holy Spirit moved. Sometimes the worship would last over an hour or two with singing and praising the Lord. People came expecting God to move. Signs, wonders and miracles were happening in this small gathering and curious unbelievers were brought into the kingdom of God.

Although the Holy Spirit was evident, there was very little teaching on Him. As a young Christian, I recall hearing about the Holy Spirit being addressed as part of the Godhead, and that He moved on the day of Pentecost. There was no teaching about having the Holy Spirit as a friend, a coach, a teacher, comforter, helper and that He is always with us if we call on Him.

It was during one of these services that I cried for hours, I knew that something was happening internally. I could not explain my feelings. Part of me felt embarrassed as my grandmother was sitting in a hammock, and others were sitting on the stairs as the church service was being carried out. There was no doubt in my heart that the Christians were serving the true and living God. This experience was new to me. And it left me confused, so I tried to meet this God through the gods I was serving. I became more dedicated; making sure I took a bath every morning, so I could stand clean before the gods. I would offer milk and food to the sun and earth. I wanted to meet this power again, but was ashamed to openly declare it. I loved my grandmother and did not want her to feel I was ungrateful to her. Our religion and culture were inseparable and I was told I could not have one without the other. Anyway, my dedication and persistency in this faith did nothing for me.

HARRISON S. MUNGAL

GODS

I BECAME CONFUSED that I was serving so many gods, yet not one of them could fill the void deep inside as the Christian God did. Two years after my first encounter, my dad became a born-again believer. The good thing about this was the fact that he dragged me to every church service he would attend. I became more intrigued, in that I knew that the Christian God was different. There was some type of energy power that became alive when the people would worship this God. I saw healing, miracles, and demon possessed set free; people were converted after they had an encounter with the Christian God. In fact over 250 Hindus became followers of Christ at a revival as a wave of the Holy Spirit was moving over our Hindu village. The disappointing thing was that I felt guilty to separate myself from my mother and grandmother. My mother at this time was undecided. She would visit the church services with my dad, but still held on to her gods. I believe she felt the same way I was feeling, that we would be considered traitors and be disowned by the rest of the family.

My belief system was a complex one and it was important to understand it. A person's belief drives them to make wise choices whether these choices are right or wrong. As a young man I was confused, however deciding to understand the gods of my mother I got myself immersed in her faith belief. I decided to give my all to these gods, obeying the rules and understanding their territorial strength in the body and the universe.

In order to understand the background and faith that I was brought up in I will share some information about a few of the various gods that I worshipped. I worshipped Annapurna, who was the god of food and cooking. This god was believed to have the ability to supply the abundance of food. This god was an incarnation of the goddess

Parvati who was the wife of Shiva. Many temples have pictures of Lord Shiva begging Annapurna for food for sustenance so he may achieve knowledge and enlightenment.

Shiva, or lord Shiva is considered to be the destroyer of the world, following the creator Brahma and Vishnu the preserver. Shiva was responsible to bring about change through death and destruction and to get rid of old habits. His first wife was Sati and second wife Parvati. When one thought of Shiva, they would focus on the snakes, which symbolized that the power of death cannot harm him and poison would have no effect on him. He is also supposed to regulate the "gunas" in the body and mind with respect to foods. Sattvic foods are considered to be fresh, juicy, nourishing, sweet, tasty and light. These foods would give the energy to the body and bring higher state of consciousness. Tamasic foods were dry, old, decaying, distasteful which consumed a large amount of energy during digestion. It has been taught that these foods brought on ignorance, pessimism and doubts. The third type of foods was called Rajastic foods. These were classified as bitter, sour, salty, hot and dry, these generated energy and vitality to the human organism. These were the foundation of motion, activities and pain.

Shiva is the god who rides on a white bull called Nandi, it is considered to be a joyful bull and sits on a tiger skin representing the mind. He sometimes is seen wearing tiger skins. He takes on many forms, sometimes with five heads which represents a combination of all energies. He dances which represents both destruction and the creation of the universe revealing the cycles of death, life and rebirth. It is said the Shiva the god of destruction crushes Apasmara the personification of ignorance. Purusha is the cosmic man who pervades the universe Purusha was dismembered by the devas – his mind is the Moon, his eyes are the Sun, and his breath is the wind and he causes forgetfulness.

Brahma was born from the navel of lord Vishnu at the end of one cycle to begin a fresh creation. He has four heads (originally five), representing the four Vedas, which are four great books or the scriptures of Hinduism. These were said to have sprung from his heads. His four heads are also said to represent the four yugas. He is bearded & his eyes are always closed in meditation. He sits on a lotus & his vahana or a Hindu vehicle, sometimes called a mount, is an animal or a mythical entity – his is the swan. In his four arms he holds the vedas, – the holy books, the kamandalam (water pot), suruva (sacrificial spoon) & a mala which is a garland of beads for counting the prayers and mantra, a repetitious prayer. He is serene and is the provider of all sources of knowledge & wisdom.

Brahma was considered to be one of the Hindu trinity; the other two were Vishnu and Shiva. He was considered to be the creator, Vishnu the God of preservation and Shiva the God of destruction. In order to create the world and produce the human race, Braham made a goddess out of himself. One half was a man and the other a woman.

Vishnu was considered to be the lord of protection, sustenance & maintenance. His consort Lakshmi is the possessor of wealth, which is a necessity for maintenance.

Goddess Lakshmi represents not only material wealth, but the wealth of grains, courage, valour, offspring, success, luxurious life, eternal bliss. Vishnu and Lakshmi thus help the souls introduced into the life cycle by Brahma to survive in the cycle of life.

Vishnu is also called Nilameghashyamalan – possessing a complexion the colour of the dark clouds. As proof that opposites attract, Vishnu's outer appearance is dark while he is associated with the santha gunam, bringing light & peace to the world. He rests on the ocean on his bed of Adisesha (serpent with 1,000 heads). Any time Lord Vishnu sees great trouble, He takes an avataram to rescue the people from evils. He is all merciful, ever rushing to serve his devotees. In the form of Mahavishnu he has four arms wielding the chakra, conch, lotus & the gadha or mace in his four arms. Some of the main avatarams of Vishnu are enumerated as the Dasavataram (10 Incarnations). He was said to be incarnated in a human form to set things right. He incarnated as fish (matsya), a turtle (Kurma), a Boar (Varaha), lion (Narasingha), dwarf(Vamana), Ram, Krishna, Buddha, and Kalki which is yet to come.

Goddess Lakshmi is the consort of Vishnu. She is considered to be the possessor of every form of wealth, fortune, prosperity, love and beauty. "Sri" is considered to be a pre-vedic deity associated with fertility, water and this deity was later merged with the vedic deity of beauty. She is the possessor of great beauty and is depicted in standing as well as in the seated postures, always on a lotus. In her hands she holds two lotuses and wears a garland of lotus. She is often depicted clad in a red saree. She is accompanied by two (sometimes four) elephants on either side either garlanding her or spraying water from pitchers. She has four arms. The two upper arms are holding lotuses, while the lower arms are normally in abhaya and varada mudras. She has on her lap, a pot overflowing with gold and other riches. She is also depicted sometimes holding the amirtha kalasam (pot of ambrosia) and bilva fruit.

Maha Kali : Kali is the goddess of dissolution and destruction. She is known for destroying ignorance, and she helps those who strive for knowledge of God. Her name means "The Black One" and the city of Calcutta is named in her honour. Kali is fearsome in appearance. She has w ild eyes, a protruding tongue, and she wields a bloody sword. Kali also holds the severed head of a demon, and she wears a belt of severed heads.

These were the main gods that would be served. Kali, a goddess is one of the wives of Shiva. She represents the wild, destructive character. She is often linked to death, wearing a necklace of human skulls, a skirt of human limbs, and with blood dripping from her weapons. At times, she can even overcome her husband. The goddess Kali, my grandmother told me was "bad". I remember she told me that this god required blood. She told me that there was a magic if the killing was done just right. The god required virgins who would not fear death. They needed to watch the knife and show no hesitancy of dying.

My aunt lived opposite a temple where blood sacrifices were offered. People would bring their animals, and as they offer their animal sacrifices, the blood of the animal would be sprayed on the individual as the life left the animal. It was said that the blood would deliver the household from evil. I was told when I visited India that a man offered his two children to this Kali god, and then offered himself. We know there is power in the blood, but only the blood of Christ as it was sinless blood.

I completed elementary school learning that there are many gods who required a person to be good and do good deeds. The more one gives to the poor, and visit the temple, the happier the gods would be. After I surrendered myself to Jesus, I felt a power inside of me whenever I went to church. This never happened in the Hindu Temple even though I was dedicated. I listed above the complicated religion from which I was taken; now the simplicity of faith in the one true God and His son Jesus gave me a calm satisfaction in life.

MY HEALING

AT THE AGE of 14 I became very ill, some said it was a demon of paralysis that came upon me paralyzing me with pain; others believed it was my "Karma" to die young and to be reincarnated. Karma represents the actions of men & women during their 'many' lives, past, present and future. According to Hindu concept, there is no short cut to liberation (moksha) and it takes innumerable rebirths, before one is finally liberated. Reincarnation provides the venue for working out the law of karma. This illness came upon me quite unexpectedly. My sister and I were playing at home one day, when suddenly I felt pain all over my body. My sister had to get a message to my mother who was visiting my grandmother approximately 8 kilometers away.

I was immediately taken to the hospital where I was diagnosed with "low hemoglobin" or a "lack of oxygen in the blood". As a child I had an accident where my lungs were punctured, the doctors advised my parents that my current condition may be related to an infection in my lungs I had earlier in life. Apparently insufficient oxygen in my blood created a series of after effects. This caused a defect in the function of the red blood cells, which exacerbated the condition of the lungs. The pressure in the lungs was high, resulting in arthritis. I experienced shortness of breath and dizzy spells which culminated in fainting spells. My entire body was in constant pain, it felt like needles were pricking me all over. My entire body was cold and my fingers were blue from the lack of circulation. The medications prescribed were not effective; in fact it aggravated the situation. I was confined to my bed and had to be lifted by my dad or a kind neighbour when it was necessary. Apparently all of this was the result of this oxygen deficiency.

My mother took me to her Hindu priest who advised her on the potions he prescribed, but nothing helped. There was a constant flow of neighbours and friends who came to assist my mother providing both moral and physical support. My body was constantly being rubbed to keep me warm, but that too was of little comfort. My mother cried everyday, as she tried to do everything she thought possible to help me. She gave me a sponge bath in bed, and she encouraged me to read the Christian Bible. Day and night I was in pain, crying non stop as the pain continued to excoriate my whole being. My mother realized that nothing was helping me so she decided to try the Christian God. The week when my situation worsened my mom sent for her brother and his wife who were the first "born again Christians" in the family. He was the last person to be consulted for anything since his conversion to Christianity. He was disowned by the rest of the family since he broke the vow of "once you were born a Hindu, you die a Hindu". My mother had consulted all her gurus or revered men of her faith. When all else failed and her faith started to waiver, the first person she thought of was her Christian brother.

As my condition worsened, well wishers, neighbours, friends and family came to visit and to offer my mother some comfort. It was during this time that my uncle and his wife arrived. They then requested everyone to leave the bedroom where I was bedridden, just my aunt and uncle were with me. When the door was firmly closed my uncle opened his Bible and began to read the 27th chapter of Psalms. As he read the Bible, I felt like the scriptures were becoming alive. I saw the scriptures painting a picture for me as it deeply penetrated my heart. After the scriptures were read, the pastor asked if I believe that Jesus can heal me. As he said this, he took me by my right hand and pulled me off the bed. The power of God was released as I felt a warm heat all over my body. I felt like someone opened a hot shower over me as the healing power of God penetrated the bone and marrow, every cell and tissue was made whole. I felt like I was dreaming, as the power of God came over me. I quickly ran outside where everyone was sitting around comforting my mother. The first reaction I saw was the people's jaws dropped as everyone stood in awe of what had happened. My mothers' face shone and I knew that she had come to the crossroad of her life to openly declare that Jesus was Lord of her life and to follow Him.

My healing was a testimony to the entire family. My mother burnt all her gods; she pulled down all her flags (jhandi) and called for a prayer meeting with the Christian church. The (Jhandi) flag usually red was planted in a corner of the front garden. It represents the spirit of the god Hanuman, a devotee of Sri Ram in the epic tale of Ramayana. The root of this religious observance came from India where the flags were installed near a temple. In the absence of the temple as in my parents' case the flag was in the corner of their property with a makeshift temple decorated with flowers and a stone where pagan prayers (puja) are offered up. These needed to be destroyed and our home sanctified by the blood of Jesus.

A new chapter in our life started with some spiritual house cleaning. We kept prayers (cottage meetings) almost every other week. I continued the prayer meeting every week inviting all our neighbours. Two other families were converted in my immediate neighbourhood and together we formed a group always inviting others.

The word spread about my healing, and the news attracted others to join our prayer group. We did not have any electricity, so we improvised using a glass bottle filled with kerosene and substituted a piece of cotton for a wick. I did not know much about the Christian God, so I used the Bible. There were so many questions thrown at me and many were unanswered. My quest was to find answers. A certain question puzzled me, it was relating to the book of Acts chapter 2 when the Holy Spirit came "like a mighty rushing wind and sat upon those who were waiting" for the promise of Jesus.

I was curious about the Holy Spirit and my questions to various pastors and church leaders were simply answered that He is the third person of the Trinity, and that He came on the day of Pentecost. These answers did not fully satisfy me as I wanted the experience as related in the Bible. Three years had gone by, and my hunger for the Holy Spirit increased, I was determined to know Him personally. I would go in the bush, some said it was the jungle, and I would call out to this Christian God. I would try to imitate how Moses called out to God during the exodus; I prayed to be filled by God's Spirit. I wanted to have an experience with the Holy Spirit, like I did when I was 7 years old. I was determined and nothing could hold me back. During these times of seeking God, my eyes were opened to the beauty of God's creation. I began to appreciate God for what He did for me. My gratitude was immense, as day by day I realized the things that God did for me, to send His only Son to die for my sins.

How different it was to serve a God who has a heart and is concerned about our relationship with Him, rather than the works. I did not have to prove to the church members that I loved God; I did not have to impress anyone that I was holy, or righteous. I had to prove nothing to the community. My life spoke for me and my commitment to the faith. I no longer had to appease God by rituals, nor wear white as a symbol of my purity. These outward gestures were not a reflection of the heart.

I became immersed in knowing more about Him and decided to dedicate my service to the God who healed me. Most people who became Christians at this time were either healed, delivered, or felt the power of God and could not deny him. My mother had spent lots of money with potions and chants as well as medicine, however she spend nothing on Christ's healing power.

POWER

"For you shall receive power after that the Holy Spirit is come upon you . . ."
Acts 1:8

WHEN I READ this scripture, it opened my heart to seek out this power. These were questions to which no one was able to give a satisfactory answer, nor would share with me how to obtain this power. I became obsessed in my search for this power. I knew that this was the power that I felt over me when I received my healing. This was the same power I felt when I was about 7 years old when I cried uncontrollably for 3 hours. I knew now that this power was real and nothing and no one in the world would persuade me differently. My entire immediate family now was saved and going to the Christian church, and the rest of the extended family could not deny what had happened. Our relationship actually became stronger as every weekend we spent time together, taking turns visiting each other's home in prayer.

As I read the Bible, I became fascinated with the power of God. I began to ask questions like; what is the purpose of this power? Why is it needed? What kind of power is the Bible talking about? How does it manifest itself?

I knew that Christ gave the church power and this power manifests itself in the humblest circumstances. I felt that the fact that this was not real among us is because the church was not lined up with the Bible. Something was amiss; maybe my expectation was too high. I know that power holds the ability to bring about change and that it can take many forms as is it measured in many ways. I was expecting to see it come and go like lightening, where everyone can notice the reality that it exists.

There was an internal hunger for this power in my life and the church of Christ as I learnt from the Bible, I saw that power was released depending on the situation or circumstances and that it can only come from God through the Holy Spirit. He was in charge and this was an essential aspect of our worship that was missing. I read how the early church operated with the Holy Spirit as they learned how to tap in to the source of this power and the function and role it played in church growth, I could not settle for anything less than what I read in the Bible.

From a very young age, I had to learn the principles that carried power. I came from a background where education meant a good job, and a good job meant that your parents would be proud. I learnt quickly that power is strength and it is needed in order to achieve much in life, be it in the work force or in the academic field. Power is the force that makes great men; it is an energy that attracts other energies. Self-will comes from innate power which is applied in the choices we make, and it affects every decision we make. It gives the corporate world and financial institutions strength and a voice to be heard and respected. Power gives authority and we decide how it is applied in our lives by using or being used by it. The power of supply and demand makes us victors or victims. Power is the position of command. Power can either build or destroy depending on how it is used. Power breaks the walls of intimidation; it creates an inner boldness that makes us challenge our limitations to step out beyond the boundaries we have set for ourselves. It helps one function in a role that is necessary to survive. It holds the capacity to bring about changes.

There are many streams from which power flows. Looking from a political sense, power is necessary for leadership. One can only imagine a leader without power; it can only be pictured as the blind leading the blind. Power is needed to lead one from one level to another. It influences behaviour of others which creates changes within the mind and heart of an individual.

When we look at the military base or the police force, we see the importance of power as it shows who is in charge. Without power, what will determine the winning of a war? Who will apply the principles to protect and serve?

Like electricity, a source is needed to generate power. Its use increases both proficiency and efficiency. The lack of it, as where I grew up, severely hampers progress, and to accomplish anything involves intensive labour. Waste is the ultimate result. The use of electricity provided refrigeration which helps in conservation by preservation, but everything comes with a sacrifice.

Types of Power

When I think of the power that exists in the world today, I remind myself that we have a touch of what originated in heaven. Firstly I'd like to think of power as superior strength, like a person who is physically strong and is capable of providing support when needed.

My first visit to the gym did not last more than 15 minutes as I felt intimidated by those who were weight lifters. I first observed trained men and women, and they radiated a sense of superiority. However, as I became acquainted with the exercise and those whom I perceived to be superior because of their strength, the myth of my perception vanished. I soon realized that they are flesh and blood with a heart like anyone else. This is how I picture the Holy Spirit to be, one who is strong and powerful, yet can be gentle like a dove. Someone who has power, and who can be intimidating when understanding is lacking, but upon acquaintance He is the most willing agreeable and tender force to work with.

Secondly, I like to view power as one of exchange. Like a worker, everyday we work with the understanding that we will receive a pay cheque. The higher the position is, the greater the pay is, to commensurate with the increased responsibility. Power comes with increased responsibility. Even in the ministry there is a chain of command. However many have opposed this method when it comes to ministry. This is because the motivating factor for such positions can be due to pride or position. The internal power is the ego, it thrives upon recognition of their accomplishments and exalted position they hold.

This brings us to the power of those in leadership. Power is a tool to be wielded for utmost effectiveness. In the hands of a wise man it benefits all but in the hands of a fool it wields death and destruction. Power reveals the true man. Men in position may fool some of the people some of the time, but not all of the people all of the time, but with power the heart and motive comes to light very quickly. Followers feel obligated and submit themselves in order to keep their job, their positions or even to gain favour with those in high places as a stepping stone to fame and fortune. Others feel threatened with having a bad reputation should they decide to challenge and fight for their rights, and may even lose their livelihood. Others just accept their lot in life as the downtrodden and lose their identity playing out their roles as non-resistant robots. The challenge of life is too enormous for them.

Everyone should recognize the power in self, for there is power in numbers and in unity, as no man is an island. The voice of the people (common folks) is a power to be reckoned with; it takes control of the power from the one that yields it. The paradox is, even though exercising the power in self is necessary to correct a situation, as a group it is imperative that each member submits to the leadership of one in the group as a representative, before changes can be implemented. Submission to leadership is giving the power or authority to act on behalf of others for their best interest. The power here is the voice of many through one. There is no autonomy but a corporate representation through one. This power is exercised only in the face of negligence or corruption. Rebellion and self-control is not power. A parallel can be drawn among believers. One takes control of his own life by being responsible of the choices he makes by which his life is governed. Like believers then submit to the authority of a leader or shepherd. The shepherd's guidelines are the doctrines prescribed in the Bible. This leadership is not autonomous but is accountable to the Holy Spirit and the sheep in His fold. The congregation does not relinquish all power to the leader but to God. Christ is the Head of His church. No leader is immune to sin. Any sign of negligence or corruption should be addressed to the elders or deacons depending on the structure of the governing body of the church.

HARRISON S. MUNGAL

Until we come to a realization that we need to make changes in our spiritual life, we will not experience the joy of being a Christian. Changes must be developed from the heart of a person. We can run to the altar for prayer after a service, or visit every guest speaker and request prayer, however if our house (body) is not clean we cannot enjoy the power of God in our lives. A believer has to take control by surrendering to the will of God, herein lies power. Every decision we make must be guided by the Holy Spirit and this will reflect positive changes. God will force no man to change. His will power will dictate his actions, when it is according to the will of God; then God will use it to fulfill His destiny in the individual. The power of God is manifested though the gift of the Holy Spirit through miracles signs and wonders. The ultimate result is that God receives the glory.

Too many are fooled by the outward appearance of an individual. They say and do all the right things in the eyes of the public but the heart is not right with God. Until we surrender to the perfect will of God to be used as He desires and not be ruled by selfish motives, we will not be used by the Almighty. It took me over 8 years to have a change of heart regarding tithing. I had a difficult time tithing 10% of my earnings, in addition to my offerings. Then there came a time when I gave all that I had with no thought of tomorrow. To my astonishment from the time I made the decision to confirm to the scriptures on tithe and offering and giving with a willing heart, the blessings I received are too numerous to mention. This brought to mind a saying of my grandmother, "When a person takes pleasure in cooking. It will yield an abundance that all will be fed".

The power between a buyer and a seller.

Although one may have a cart full of groceries, it does not belong to them until it has been paid for. This is called the transfer of power. That goes for every item we purchase. If someone would take an item that has not been paid for, the transaction is illegal and it is called theft. Similarly, believers attempt to claim the gifts of the Holy Spirit without being willing to pay the price through making a sacrifice. Many men and women of God expect to bring healing, salvation and deliverance to the world, without a passion for prayer, worship and fellowship with the Holy Spirit. They seem to think that God is obligated to perform as they fancy. Many use someone else's blueprint for their own and expect the same results. The unfortunate thing is no one knows the personal sacrifice of the leaders; the prayer and supplication presented to the throne of God, not to mention the vision behind their success. No one can flow in someone else's anointing, nor can we copy someone else's ministry. Each of us who have a call upon our lives has it at a cost; some greater than others. Personal sacrifice is the cost that moves God. We may experience a move of God as a result of other people's faith and prayer; however the minister is accountable as the power rests on him.

Too many are in the ministry to demonstrate that their leadership style is the reason for their success. These so called successes don't last, the church or ministry is not ours but God's. All attempts to show the world our power is futile unless Jesus is the head directing us through the Holy Spirit. When we relinquish our will to God and allow the Holy Spirit to flow through us, we will experience significant progress in the ministry. All living things grow. The body of Christ grows when it is healthy. Anything unhealthy will be cast out, as it irritates the body.

Politicians rely on the support of their constituents whose votes place them in a position to act on their behalf representing their rights. The people have given them the power. Many times that power has been acquired by emotional speeches and manipulative promises. It is the people that transferred their power over to him/her. They plea and beg for the votes, every ballot is precious, but when the polls are closed, the successful candidate reveals his real motive. Promises are shamelessly broken and the electorate is powerless to do anything, at least not until the next election, unlike politicians, the Holy Spirit works with us with the intention that we will support the work of Christ. He will not leave us neither will He turn His back on us. We will forever become employed with Him, as He lifts up the name of Jesus.

The power of the Holy Spirit flows over us, energizing us and directing that energy to fulfill the will of God. He is the power source of God. He was with the Father in beginning of time, and still is and will continue to be. His power is endless and inexhaustible. He also works through us, with healings, miracles, signs and wonders. God's work is accomplished upon this earth through the Holy Spirit operating in us. Our commitment to God is demonstrated though the fruit of the spirit, and we reap the benefits by the gifts of the Spirit which brings glory to God. It is through us that others see the work of God; He makes it known that this power cannot be acquired by the flesh. He holds the power to direct our path and gives us the ability to change our world.

The power of ownership exists at different levels. We see the power we hold as we compare ourselves with others. We try to "keep up with the Jones" with materialistic things. People like to compare themselves with others. This elevates to another level, where countries compete for power. In this territorial struggle for power countries test their strength by challenging others or by capitalizing on their weaknesses. The ones that pay the price are the subjects of those countries. Innocent blood is shed for vain glory. Your test of loyalty is measured by your willingness to be patriotic and stand for your country regardless of the cause. Fatherless children are deprived of a father and robbed of a comfortable home. Widows have to fend for themselves to earn a living or they make unsound judgement in remarrying to fill the financial void in their lives. The compensation for deaths and amputees is misery. Family life is rarely the same. This is especially sad when the aggressor's motive is selfish and senseless.

In the Christian world, there is a daily war in the spiritual realm. Christ is interceding daily together with His followers. The battle has never stopped since Satan fell. The battle is always raging. Satan the aggressor is out to kill and destroy, death and destruction is his only aim. Like the countries at war, humans are caught up in the battle and his struggle for power. His fight is not with us, but with God for it is only though us that he can get to God. We carry God's image which he is trying to deface. Like the politicians he makes false promises causing us to sin. He hurts God by hurting that which God loves.

Like countries at war who enlist soldiers for battle we too have to be prepared for battle. Like a soldier we too have to wear armour to defend ourselves and have the ammunition or sword ready to fight. Unlike the soldier in battle the Christian fight ends with life not death. The family is victorious, not defeated by this conquest. The cause is righteous and our inheritance secure. Instead of sadness and misery, there is joy and peace. There is a constant power struggle even though the devil knows that he was defeated by the death of Christ. What is bad is that even though Satan has been defeated he still tries to capitalize on our weaknesses and influence us with the lies he has been feeding mankind with since the fall of Adam.

Many people have an insatiable need for power and Satan likes to give the impression that he has the ability to deliver. The believer has the power of God in him/her and "greater is He that is in me than he that is in the world". Satan is no match for God. When we understand this we will live victorious lives. The Bible makes it clear that "the earth is the Lord's and the fullness thereof"; we are God's creation, part of the fullness of the earth. We were born to conquer but not of self. We see the power in the law of the land, a soldier enlisted must go to battle or face imprisonment, a deserter is court-marshalled. Every infraction has a penalty and every action earns a consequence. God also has established His laws as a guide for us to follow. We either obey or disobey and reap the consequences for our action. Breaking His law is more dangerous for us, compared to breaking the law of man.

With this we see how parents who hold power in relationship to their children will attempt all means possible to see that their child continues their education. The power or authority from the parent, teacher, friend or colleague towards the child can be overwhelming at times. However if the motives are right, we see well educated children as the end result. The Holy Spirit can take the form of a teacher, a friend and a colleague and His motives are always right. He wants us to become the best we can be. He does not give up on us as He focuses on strengthening our weaknesses and polishing our strengths.

As a father of seven, my role is to make sure that I train our children in the way of the Lord. Our hope is that each one of our children will become the person God designed them to be. In reaching that goal, we play our part, by providing the support needed. Part of which is educational support. We motivate our children by allowing them to chose an event they would like to attend anywhere in Canada, providing they accomplished all "A's" at the end of their semester. We encouraged them with a financial gift for each "A", as well as an improvement in their grades. We have also promised them a trip to any island when accepted to a University. We have taught our children how to study and provide whatever support needed for projects. In addition, I have also used the strategy where each morning, each child who has been struggling with their grades, does additional homework for me to correct. I spend quality time with each child taking them out for coffee or a soft drink and making it known to them that they are special. Our expectation is for them to do their best. Without forcing them to achieve academic goals, we have seen them maintain an over 80 average, or increase in their grade level. We hold the power but do not abuse it.

I have learned this principle from the Holy Spirit. He teaches us all things as His intentions are to see that we progress and fulfil the divine plan, purpose, and destiny God has designed for us. In every service He enters with power as a reminder that He can do more. He looks to see how His power is operated through us and that we don't abuse it or give the impression that we have the power. He carefully looks for the maturity and the ability to handle more. As much is given, much is required.

The purpose of these types of power is to make others yield by reason; however some people use fear as a psychological force, which make others feel threatened. Although power can make others feel like they are being punished, or helpless, it creates a guideline and discipline, developing character and experience. There is a cost to maintaining and implementing power. The greater the cost, the more experience is developed creating an increase of self confidence and boldness. These characteristics automatically give the signal as to who is in charge and who is leading the way.

We should strive to have integrative power which binds our hearts together. This is a power like agape love, it binds humans together. Although this type of power is incongruent with love and kindness of humans, it is the key to see faith released and the power of the Holy Spirit manifested. The Holy Spirit has sanctioned this type of power over God's people. It brings unity, loyalty and respect within the body of Christ. The Holy Spirit has given many incentives to have this particular type of power within the Church; however we either take advantage of His blessings or ignore them.

When integrative power crumbles, we see conflict within the body of Christ including the local church. The cost becomes enormous to bring it back together; however there is always hope in the Holy Spirit for those who are walking with Him, to develop this power. In order for people to act effectively, there must be an understanding of each others needs, interest, motives and the ability to agree to disagree. There must be an open line of communication with the Holy Spirit and each other, as well as seeking forgiveness and becoming accountable to each other. This will reduce conflict and develop integrative power.

With this responsibility comes the power of persuasion where our attitude can be changed. As we collaborate with each other, the power of the Holy Spirit can extend to greater territories. When the church is lacking power, the enemy has no concerns as power took back what the devil has stolen.

ALL HAIL THE POWER . . .

THREE YEARS LATER after being healed, I could no longer settle for a good feeling, I wanted more. I wanted to have the presence of God constantly over my life and this became my drive. I knew that the power of God existed and I knew it was for the church, however could not understand why I was feeling empty. The Bible stated that we will become wells, then a spring, and during this time of my life, I felt like my well was dry.

Coming from a society where there was no running water, I knew the importance of cherishing a well or a spring. We had a well dug to supply water for my grandmother's vegetable garden which eventually became empty and full of garbage, and I was seeing myself to be like this well. I had learnt from my grandmother that the well dug in her land was used to supply water to the few neighbours in the area as well as her crop she planted, which also was her source of income. The well was lined with stones to prevent it from collapsing. I felt that the stones in my spiritual well were crumbling inside of me.

My sister and I would walk for over an hour carrying a bucket in each hand to bring water from the main public tap; otherwise we had no drinking water. The well went dry as time went by and no one bothered to clear it out. My grandmother at this time no longer planted her vegetable garden, so there was not too much of a need, except for ourselves. Many of us can be like a well, where God is at the inside; we have a measure of the Holy Spirit at the inside of us, however only when we become springs will we see living water flowing out of us. We can become dependent on others for our spiritual source of strength, or attempt to draw from others; however we can only have a taste from each other's wells. In order for us to produce spiritual life, we need to start with a well.

My mom had told me about a spring we had in our land, which eventually dried up. She shared with me, explaining that when she was a little girl they would all drink from this spring. This spring was a place where water flowed out of the ground under its own volition, either as a result of gravity or hydrostatic pressure. Unlike a well where the water had to be pumped out, the spring flows out of the ground into the surface, and the water is always pure as most would say. However there are springs with mineralized water, in which case the spring is then termed a mineral or salt spring. This spring drew pure water, like we have in water bottles today. The water was always cold and tasty. I remember living in Croatia and drinking from a river which had a spring flowing into it. The water was cold and soothing to satisfy the thirst.

My mother explained how the water would seep through the soil and yet there was no discernable outlet. The spring was noted for its coolness and its pure taste. She shared how people from everywhere would come and fill their vessels as it was used for drinking water. I wanted to be like a spring with the ability to have the power like the water at the surface of my life, rather than inside of me. I wanted the world to know that I serve the living God, and that everyone I come across, will want to hear about His love towards humanity. Just like the spring that went dry, some of our spiritual springs have gone dry and we live by the experience of what it use to be like when the Holy Spirit was flowing out of us. God never gives up on us and we should not give up on ourselves.

There was a determination to seek the face of God with a hope that my well will become a spring of living water. Jesus mentioned to the women at the well that He will give her rivers of living water, and I wanted this living water.

Isaiah 55:6 which states *"Seek the LORD while He may be found, Call upon Him while He is near."*

I began to ask myself questions such as: Does this mean that there will be a time that I will not be able to find this God? If I call on Him, does this mean He will draw near to me? Scriptures like James 4:8 *"Draw nigh to God, and he will draw nigh to you. Cleanse your hands, ye sinners; and purify your hearts, ye double minded."*

I would read thinking that God would be around only temporarily and that if I wanted to draw near to Him, I needed to purify my heart, I needed to call upon His name. My biggest question was how this was possible to meet the Christian God. I would even tell God that we have an appointment at such and such a time and I would go expecting to see someone or feel His presence. I was taught in my previous faith that God can make Himself known in any shape, size or form. I really did not know what I was expecting, however I knew internally, every time I met with God, something happened to me. I grew more secure and became internally stronger.

It came to a point in my early walk with the Lord that I felt it was time to meet this Christian God. It was time for an encounter with Him again. I wanted to meet the Holy Spirit, I wanted to be filled with His presence, I wanted to experience what the early church experienced and nothing was going to stand in the way. I wanted the water of life to flow out from deep within. It is the living water that will show the reality of Christ in my life.

Desperation drove me to go to church often, spending time fasting and seeking every opportunity of quality time in prayer. Early one Sunday morning, I was up at the altar when the most beautiful thing happened to me. As the church was worshipping, I began to feel the same power I experienced when I was healed. The warmth, the love, the comfort and the joy all around me, created an internal hunger for more. I could not contain myself; it would be an encounter that would change my life for a lifetime.

All Hail the Power . . .

During this Sunday morning church service we were singing a hymn "All Hail The Power Of Jesus Name and Crown Him Lord of All", when suddenly I saw the power of the blood of Christ. I saw for the first time, that I needed to crown the God who died for my sins; an innocent God who deserved all the honour and glory. The hymn suddenly became alive and opened my eyes to see heaven open and angels falling before the throne of God, crowning Him Lord of All. As I continued to sing this hymn the words became a part of me and my worship of my King. The words became my heart's prayer and stirred the power of God deep inside of me.

My entire body began trembling like a leaf, especially my left side. As my left leg began to shake uncontrollably, I became self conscious of my situation and felt embarrassed. However, the joy internally did not allow my flesh to stop praising God for who He is and what He had done in my life. My joy was full, my peace was full, and the love that came into my heart has never left me.

As I was being empowered by this majestic power of God, I felt my entire inside becoming new. I felt the cleansing like a dirty rag soaked in bleach, I was becoming clean. This felt like it was going on for hours until I eventually fell to the floor, my entire body felt like jelly. It was like I had fallen on soft cushions and my legs seem to be falling asleep on me. I was oriented, yet confused as to what was happening, only to realize that it all happened in about fifteen minutes.

I did not know what to make of this experience at that time. In my embarrassment, part of me felt that I was being punished and my fall was a result of that. Another part of me did not care, as something wonderful had happened internally. The reaction I received from some of the congregation after the service was "God really did a work in you", others said, "You are on the right track". Some could not believe that there was an actual move in the church as we did not see the Holy Spirit moving in the church for a while.

My determination to have the well inside of me spring alive was showing progressively and I did not intend to stop pushing for more. I did not speak in tongues as most people would, however my tongue was rolling without syllables. The week I was touched by Holy Spirit, was the same week the church was in a week of prayer and fasting. Everyday that week I was in church and everyday, something was happening internally. I started to speak one sentence in tongues and it became repetitive, until that heavenly language grew. I eventually felt the well springing up from deep within me as my relationship with the Holy Spirit grew. Jude 20 became a light to me. I was building myself up in the most holy faith, praying in the Holy Spirit everyday, every spare moment I had. I did not want to quit. I was consumed with a hunger to know Him more and more.

RECEIVING THE PROMISE

WHAT I HAVE learned from desiring to be filled with the Holy Spirit is that no one can make it happen for you. Being filled with the Holy Spirit may be repetitive, but there is one baptism of the Holy Spirit. Once you are baptized with the Holy Spirit, you are given the privilege to be filled every time you meet with Him. The Holy Spirit becomes your energy, your fluid for the fire in your life.

> *"And when they had prayed, the place was shaken where they were assembled together; and they were all filled with the Holy Ghost, and they spake the word of God with boldness."* Acts. 4:31

There is no mechanical procedure involved in receiving the Holy Spirit. It is a gift given by God to an open-hearted and hungry believer. It is not necessary to have any deep theological understanding of the baptism of the Holy Spirit. Like the Gentiles at Caesarea who had almost little or no understanding of the Holy Spirit when they received Him. I realized all we need to do is to surrender, yielding our whole heart to God, desiring to live righteously and to forsake all sin.

Even though we may never believe that we are holy enough to earn the Holy Spirit. He is a gift of God (Acts 8:20). We need to ask God, and keep on asking until it happens. I was praying for an encounter with the Holy Spirit weeks prior to being filled with Him (Luke 11:9-13, James 4:2). Asking breaks the pride we hold internally. Remember the Bible made it clear that tongues is a sign that will follow those who believe.

There had been several occasions, when I encouraged my daughters to ask for extra napkins at a restaurant, or even to return a bill for being over charged, they found it difficult and embarrassing. We have to learn to ask in order to receive; we need to believe that it is God's desire to fill us with His Holy Spirit. We should not be seeking tongues or an experience but though the Grace of God we receive His free gift to us. When God starts moving, we need to become willing receptacles for whatever He is about to pour into us, whether it be to speak in tongues, a word of knowledge or to prophecy. He moves on those who are available and willing to conform to His will.

We must lose ourselves in Him surrendering to His will, there is nothing forced or mechanical, or to compare with others. God is able to give to each individual a different tongue, like He did for the early church. Our priority is to become consumed in praising and worshipping God from the heart, oblivious to what others may think or feel, instead of giving Him lip service. When one receives God's gift, it is unique and it holds the power of its purpose. It does not sound like empty words. Many times people attempt to work up their emotions or suppress their emotions; however it does not bring the gift to us. Our own effort or fleshly impression will not bring the gift. Faith and total surrender to the Lord opens the doors for the Holy Spirit to give His gift.

My passion is to live the experience and capture the joy of being filled with the Holy Spirit as on the day of Pentecost. I want to live the real thing and I am conscious that the gift is not given because I am a Christian, but because I earnestly want to become stronger in my faith in Christ. I was willing to do whatever it took to have this gift materialize, I soon realized that I did not need to pay any penance, or wait a period of time to be eligible for the gift of tongues. I did not have to impress God by being a good person to qualify for this gift. In fact my most noble attempts to procure this gift are insignificant to God.

Trying to imitate someone or to speak gibberish will not endow me with this power. I needed to make a commitment to God and yield to Him. A vessel willing to do His will. I might thirst after this gift but only if God sees me worthy will He let the Holy Spirit loosen my faltering tongue to this beloved and much sought after language.

There were many incidents when the anointing was strong in church; I felt that the Holy Spirit was resting upon me. However, a lack of boldness to open my mouth and let these unknown words given by the Lord pour forth from my inner being inhibited the Holy Spirit from flowing through me. We subconsciously resist the Holy Spirit by reverting in our native tongue. Ears cannot comprehend the sound and the tongue is untrained to deliver, just like any other foreign language. When the Holy Spirit is upon us and unfamiliar words are coming from our inner most being in faith we should bring forth the words in sound. The more we speak in this heavenly language, the more our spirit will develop.

The difference between learning a language and the gift of the heavenly language is that it is not necessarily a repetitive language. Depending on the situation and the recipient or interpreter of this message, the Holy Spirit yields His power accordingly, if we do not have the gift of interpretation then the Holy Spirit will use us as the vessel to proclaim the word and empower someone else to complete the message. These oracles in the church are very potent in building faith: and we build ourselves in our most holy faith (Jude 20).

We have to come to the realization that we can only speak in tongues as the Holy Spirit gives the utterance (Acts 2:4), when this happens, after it happens then and only then we begin a journey of fulfilment. We are no longer the same; we become bold, enthusiastic and are driven by a desire to bring the reality of Christ to our world. Our passion is Christ and Him crucified, He who rose again and will be returning for His church. We will begin to see through the eyes of the Holy Spirit and we gladly submit ourselves to His guidance.

I had difficulty yielding my tongue to God because I assumed that the Holy Spirit will overpower and empower me in this language transition. Then to my amazement, the Holy Spirit was playing the role of a coach and I had to submit to His teaching, the effort on my part was to obey what I was told and in faith do the unthinkable regardless of who was around and what they would feel or think of me. I had to surrender my physical to accomplish the spiritual. Holding back and feeling discouraged will only be hindrances in accomplishing my instructions. Total capitulation will propel these wonderful words like an uncapped spring brings forth the beauty and wonder of this imprisoned desire. Resistance will continue to keep me suppressed and frustrated. My concern over worldly things will inhibit my progress and until I learn who is in control this will not be manifested. This will be an expression to the Lord and not to man.

The same principle applies during our decision for salvation. Some of us become more emotional than others, and may express themselves in a different fashion than others, carefree to what the world thinks of us. Being filled with the Holy Spirit is like consummating a marriage, all reticence, self-consciousness, hang-ups, and inhibitions are over ridden by the strong resolve to answer to the immediate call. The magnetic power of intimacy intensifies as we are drawn closer to Him, and suddenly we throw all cares away and acquiesce to a force stronger than our will power. We become weak under this power and the fight to struggle no longer has a hold over the physical. The communication lines once established gives us the new freedom to soar freely with Him.

BAPTISM

MANY CHRISTIANS EMBRACE their faith in Jesus Christ and stop there. They are comfortable in the knowledge that they are now saved and their salvation is secure, but fail to realize that there is more to this wonderful relationship. As in a marriage, every day we discover new things about our spouse and this never stops until the day we die. Similarly, every day with Jesus and the Holy Spirit is sweeter than the day before. It's a journey that never ends, and as we develop this relationship we are constantly discovering His love and majesty, to which we have free access and He is willing to share with us by coaching us along the way.

Many Christians have been in the faith for years and have cheated themselves of enjoying this wonderful adventure. Complacency is the major reason in immobilizing the work of the Holy Spirit. We become insensitive to its stirrings and promptings, many do not realize He will not over ride our free will, we have to become active participants and ask Him to teach and guide us. Instead we are frozen in time and there is no progress until something drastic occurs in our lives to awaken a new consciousness. Remember the enemy will supply all the reasons why we do not have to thrive for further involvement. This is the beginning of a slippery road to adhering to the world and self, and is a sign that we have to struggle against and overcome the battle within.

The baptism of the Holy Spirit is the right to every born again believer the world over. It is a confirmation that He is omnipresent, and a sign of His seal on every advocate professing Jesus as Lord over his/her life. We then become recipients of His fruit by which we are recognized by the world. As the fruit of the spirit is developed in us, we receive His gifting, giving us the ability to overcome the devil and demonstrate to the world who we serve.

According to our availability we are empowered with gifts of the spirit by which healing, miracles, signs and wonders continue as a confirmation that God is alive as He was in the early church and through these wonders souls are drawn to Him as they behold His Glory. It is God's plan that lives are revived through these gifts, but God will only do this through committed men and women in service to Him.

We are identified as Christians by our baptism, through this new identity we are embraced in the body of Christ, to function as a member of that body. Our spirit communes with the Holy Spirit in fulfilling our purpose in that body. The Holy Spirit is common to all believers; no one has a monopoly or freer access than others. It is up to us to foster that relationship and grow in Him. We all have a unique place as part of the body so that the five fold ministry established by the early church can function in love and unity to bring glory to God.

Our purpose as individuals is to praise and worship our creator. In recognizing His love for us and what He has done to bring us back to Him, we have a commitment to share this with others who do not know of this great sacrifice and our value to Him. If we truly appreciate the price paid in redeeming us from this dark world we would have a passion to spread this great news. The Great commission for every believer then is to evangelize, as we pledge ourselves in this service we will also be challenged by the needs of those we meet. He commanded His disciples not to be afraid, but to lay hands on the sick, spend quality time in prayer and fasting, confessing Christ and Him crucified. There was an internal fire, a boldness, enthusiasm and power to stand up to complete the call of God upon their lives.

Not everyone who is baptized in the Holy Spirit speaks in tongues, as tongues are a sign, and not 'the' sign. So regardless if one is speaking in tongues or not, once they are baptized in the Holy Spirit, they move into another level of faith. It is an act of the Holy Spirit. We are baptized *in* the Holy Spirit and not *by* the Holy Spirit. (Acts 1:5, 1 Cor. 12:13) The baptism by the Holy Spirit brings a new union, a new position in Christ and a new association with the believers in Christ. It is the Christian standard; it is our identity and a free gift given by God. On the other hand, we should remember that being baptized in the Holy Spirit is not a requirement for salvation. In Acts 16:30-31 shared about the Philippian jailer who asked "Sirs what must I do to be saved?". Paul answered, "Believe on the Lord Jesus Christ."

"Praying always with prayer and supplication in the Spirit and watching thereunto with all perseverance and supplication for all saints." Eph. 6:18

"Likewise the Spirit also helps our weaknesses: for we know not what we should pray for as we ought: but the Spirit Himself makes intercession for us with groanings which cannot be uttered. Now He that searches the hearts knows what the mind of the Spirit is, because he makes intercession for the saints according to the will of God." Ro. 8:26-27NKJV

HOLY SPIRIT MY COACH

It is an erroneous belief among many, that Christians automatically receive the baptism of the Holy Spirit at conversion, no one can be converted without the act of the Holy Spirit, but being baptised by Him requires a deeper level of relationship. Some advocate that we receive the Holy Spirit at water baptism while others presume we have the Holy Spirit when we speak in tongues. The Holy Spirit is a person; He can be a stranger to some of us because we have not embraced Him and until we involve Him in our lives, we will not get to know Him fully. There must be a conscious effort on our part in requesting His help and His guidance, welcoming Him in all activities of our life. When we are baptized in Him, there is visible evidence of His presence in the person's life.

> "... they were all filled with the Holy Ghost, and began to speak with other tongues, as the Spirit gave them utterance." (Acts 2:1-4)

Precription for Baptism

The scriptures attest to this observable manifestation as outlined below.

> "I indeed baptize you with water unto repentance, but He who is coming after me is mightier than I, whose sandals I am not worthy to carry. He will baptize you with the Holy Spirit and fire. His winnowing fan is in His hand, and He will thoroughly clean out His threshing floor, and gather His wheat into the barn; but He will burn up the chaff with unquenchable fire." **Matthew 3:11-12 NKJV**

> "And John bore witness, saying, 'I saw the Spirit descending from heaven like a dove, and He remained upon Him. I did not know Him, but He who sent me to baptize with water said to me, 'Upon whom you see the Spirit descending, and remaining on Him, this is He who baptizes with the Holy Spirit." **John 1:32-33NKJV**

> "He who believes in Me, as the Scripture has said, out of his heart will flow rivers of living water. But this He spoke concerning the Spirit, whom those believing in Him would receive; for the Holy Spirit was not yet given, because Jesus was not yet glorified" **John 7:38-39 NKJV**

> "These things I have spoken to you while being present with you. But the Helper, the Holy Spirit, whom the Father will send in My name, He will teach you all things, and bring to your remembrance all things that I said to you". **John 14:25-26 NKJV**

> "And I will pray the Father, and He will give you another Helper, that He may abide with you forever – the Spirit of truth, whom the world cannot receive, because

it neither sees Him nor knows Him; but you know Him, for He dwells with you and will be in you." **John 14:16-17 NVKJ**

"But when the Helper comes, whom I shall send to you from the Father, the Spirit of truth who proceeds from the Father, He will testify of Me." **John 15:26 NKJV**

"Nevertheless I tell you the truth. It is to your advantage that I go away; for if I do not go away, the Helper will not come to you; but if I depart, I will send Him to you. And when He has come, He will convict the world of sin, and of righteousness, and of judgment: of sin, because they do not believe in Me; of righteousness, because I go to My Father and you see Me no more; of judgment, because the ruler of this world is judged. I still have many things to say to you, but you cannot bear them now. However, when He, the Spirit of truth, has come, He will guide you into all truth; for He will not speak on His own authority, but whatever He hears He will speak; and He will tell you things to come. He will glorify Me, for He will take of what is Mine and declare it to you. All things that the Father has are Mine. Therefore I said that He will take of Mine and declare it to you". **John 16:7-15 NKJV**

"And being assembled together with them, He commanded them not to depart from Jerusalem, but to wait for the Promise of the Father, "which," He said, "you have heard from Me; for John truly baptized with water, but you shall be baptized with the Holy Spirit not many days from now." Therefore, when they had come together, they asked Him, saying, "Lord, will You at this time restore the kingdom to Israel?" And He said to them, "It is not for you to know times or seasons which the Father has put in His own authority. But you shall receive power when the Holy Spirit has come upon you; and you shall be witnesses to Me in Jerusalem, and in all Judea and Samaria, and to the end of the earth.". **Acts 1:4-9 NKJV**

"And He said to them, "Go into all the world and preach the gospel to every creature. He who believes and is baptized will be saved; but he who does not believe will be condemned. And these signs will follow those who believe: In My name they will cast out demons; they will speak with new tongues; they will take up serpents; and if they drink anything deadly, it will by no means hurt them; they will lay hands on the sick, and they will recover. So then, after the Lord had spoken to them, He was received up into heaven, and sat down at the right hand of God. And they went out and preached everywhere, the Lord working with them and confirming the word through the accompanying signs. Amen." **Mark 16:15-20 NKJV**

"This Jesus God has raised up, of which we are all witnesses. Therefore being exalted to the right hand of God, and having received from the Father the promise of the Holy Spirit, He poured out this which you now see and hear". **Acts 2:32-33 NKJV**

"Then Peter said to them, "Repent, and let every one of you be baptized in the name of Jesus Christ for the remission of sins; and you shall receive the gift of the Holy Spirit. For the promise is to you and to your children, and to all who are afar off, as many as the Lord our God will call."." **Acts 2:38-39 NKJV**

"And Ananias went his way and entered the house; and laying his hands on him he said, "Brother Saul, the Lord Jesus, who appeared to you on the road as you came, has sent me that you may receive your sight and be filled with the Holy Spirit." Immediately there fell from his eyes something like scales, and he received his sight at once; and he arose and was baptized."." **Acts 9:17-18 NKJV**

"While Peter was still speaking these words, the Holy Spirit fell upon all those who heard the word. And those of the circumcision who believed were astonished, as many as came with Peter, because the gift of the Holy Spirit had been poured out on the Gentiles also. For they heard them speak with tongues and magnify God. Then Peter answered, "Can anyone forbid water, that these should not be baptized who have received the Holy Spirit just as we have? And he commanded them to be baptized in the name of the Lord. Then they asked him to stay a few days."." **Acts 10:44-48 NKJV**

"And as I began to speak, the Holy Spirit fell upon them, as upon us at the beginning. Then I remembered the word of the Lord, how He said, 'John indeed baptized with water, but you shall be baptized with the Holy Spirit. If therefore God gave them the same gift as He gave us when we believed on the Lord Jesus Christ, who was I that I could withstand God?" **Acts 11:15-17 NKJV**

"And when they had prayed, the place where they were assembled together was shaken; and they were all filled with the Holy Spirit, and they spoke the word of God with boldness. Now the multitude of those who believed were of one heart and one soul; neither did anyone say that any of the things he possessed was his own, but they had all things in common. And with great power the apostles gave witness to the resurrection of the Lord Jesus. And great grace was upon them all". **Acts 4:31-33 NKJV**

"And the disciples were filled with joy and with the Holy Spirit". **Acts 13:52 NKJV**

"Then the churches throughout all Judea, Galilee, and Samaria had peace and were edified. And walking in the fear of the Lord and in the comfort of the Holy Spirit, they were multiplied". **Acts 9:31 NKJV**

"But you, beloved, building yourselves up on your most holy faith, praying in the Holy Spirit, keep yourselves in the love of God, looking for the mercy of our Lord Jesus Christ unto eternal life". **Jude 1:20-21 KNJV**

HARRISON S. MUNGAL

MY FIRST SERMON

THESE SCRIPTURES SPOKE volumes to me; with this understanding I developed an urge to know God even more. I had one motivation and one desire, and that was for God to use me to reignite the fires which were present in the early church and that had been rekindled during the days of revivalists and reformists. To confound the wise of this world as to the wisdom of God and to mesmerize them with the conquering aspect of this vanquished force active in us. His awesomeness in transforming lives and bringing to subjection the work of the enemy is in the healing of the nations. Men with like passions allowing themselves to be used in this awe-inspiring work, as Paul submitted himself without reservation. It is possible today as it was then for men and women to perpetuate this incredible phenomenon, He is asking "who shall I send"?

We have to stand up and be counted as we make a case for Christ. Unbelievers need something overwhelming and splendid to look forward to before they are willing to change their lifestyle. I want to be a part of this movement; I want to be to avail myself. I am ready to commit and I feel God is working in others for this great awakening so profound that it will annihilate the powers of this world. God is real, we need to be reassured of His presence, and the world needs to see His work in and through us. I see the power of making people happy, the joy that fills the throne of God.

As mentioned earlier, after my healing I started a bible study once a week at my home. Our improvised glass kerosene lamps made of glass bottles provided light during our service. The simplicity of this setting did not keep the Holy Spirit from working among us, but there was a missing link, connecting the Bible with man. Even though I was young there was a burning desire to know this power in a more intimate way. Being a Hindu, where we had so many rituals to initiate the gods to react, I had a discipline imbedded in me from my early childhood. We lived in expectation of but that was all, false hopes. Now that I have come to a faith in which I am a participant, it brought me to the full realization of this power. I was energized with anticipation and willing to do whatever it takes.

My quest was not a fantasy, because I had all the faith that God would not disappoint me. I now know of a power which triumphs over evil, that which raised Christ from the dead. I longed for a relationship with this power by which Christ was led, while He was on this earth. He astounded the crowds and the religious leaders with His miracle ministry, and He imparted this power to His disciples and enabled them to do even greater things than He did. I am amazed that more Christians do not comprehend the power they have in Jesus. When I grasped this truth I became conscious of the ability my saviour has endorsed to the believer. It seems that believers don't fully grasp the authority they have inherited through Jesus Christ.

I systematically looked to leaders in the faith to guide me in this path I so desperately sought. I was perplexed at their complacency about this wonderful gift from God. It bordered on doubt that it can happen to them or if they were worthy to receive that which He promised. For me on the other hand, this realization enlightened at what God can do through man. Maybe my mind can only comprehend the simple truth before me because I took this almighty creator God at His word.

In my pursuit I started studying and acquainting myself with the ways of God. I did not give up when my questions were seemingly unanswered. I persevered for three years, never getting discouraged until finally it happened. The songs we sang about the Holy Spirit were about His purpose in our lives, but there was no teaching on having a relationship with Him, that He is the power source of God who came to earth establish His Church.

In as much as my experience was an end in itself; it was not the end of the Spirit working in me. The experience led to another, the Holy Spirit was prompting me to launch out in the field of evangelizing the word of God. I never considered evangelizing, nor should I say I never connected evangelizism with the Holy Spirit as I linked speaking in tongues with Him. I never had a passion for winning souls until I was filled with the Holy Spirit. It would appear that it was the key to unveil my eyes to see the need for bringing souls to Christ, but once this was birthed in me, my Coach the Holy Spirit was there to guide me. He took away all fear of the intimidating prospect of going up to people great and small to tell them of the Lord. In fact it was easy, my life was a testimony. I was not fazed by the possibility of immense rejection. Rather I felt sympathy for those who would not heed the message of salvation.

I once had a vision of people from every culture, every race, great and small standing before God. They were all worshiping Him in oneness. As the spirit of God moved, they were in unity like a wheat field blowing with the wind in one accord. Everyone was in unity worshipping the Lord. Like the wheat I also saw many broken as broken stalks, crying out for help for different situations in life. Among them were the hungry, the abused, the sick, and the lonely. Through the worship of the strong believers, the weak and downtrodden were revitalized and strengthened. As the power of God saturated the place many were touched by the healing and others received strength to go on living as they proceeded to the altar. What a glorious sight to see a mosaic of people, people from every nationality and all walks of life coming together in oneness of voice, purpose and desire.

The day I was filled with the Holy Spirit, one of the pastors of the church was moved to invite me and a friend to the front. As we came up to the altar he prophesied that God had anointed me to be an evangelist and that many souls would come to know the power of the cross under that anointing. His prophetic message was also on my life and other areas of work which the Lord had prepared for me. There was a tendency for me to doubt all that he was saying because the gravity of the message was too much to take in and part of me could not comprehend fully the force of a prophetic message. I knew in some small measure it was a confirmation to my experience with the Lord when I was 14 years old. When the prophetic word was released I felt like someone placing a coat over me, equipping for the battle.

Not many days later, my friend and I met and he suggested that we should go out to evangelize. His theory was, if this prophecy was from God, positive results will ensue. I decided not to reveal what had happened to me at age fourteen to anyone. I did not want anyone to have unreasonable expectations from me because of what had happened. Besides, I considered this encounter with God to be personal. At my friend's insistence I felt pressured to prove that the pastor had heard from God. I did not feel equipped to go out and preach the gospel message, and I did not share my feelings with my friend for I was unsure what to do.

That weekend we went out evangelising. At the very first home we went to a mother and her four children gave their hearts to the Lord. At the second home the owner gave his heart to the Lord. I was beginning to think that my friend may have set me up; this was too good to be true, seeing people accepting the Lord without any resistance. When another welcomed the Lord at the third home I was dumbfounded, was this real? I realized this was the power of God in action. I became bold and enthusiastic for the Lord. I needed no pep talk, I went to gatherings in the neighbourhood where boys and young men would be smoking marijuana, and I would tell them of Christ and what he could do for them. The hold of scepticism that was on me was released and I enjoyed a freedom as I never had before.

I started to preach on street corners, at street meetings, prayer meetings, special services, and wherever the opportunity would grant me the pleasure. I invited everyone I met to church. I was not a victim of fear and my enthusiasm was contagious. This confidence had its moments of doubts, I did have moments of an attack of butterflies in my stomach upon approaching a group, however, the moment I opened my mouth, my self confidence was reinstated. There was never a problem speaking on a one to one basis; it was the crowd with which I had to overcome the barrier of apprehension. It was an area I needed to conqueror and not to be conquered.

HARRISON S. MUNGAL

My First Sermon

Early one Monday morning during the summer, I was sitting in my bedroom praying and reading the Word of God, I felt that presence again, the presence of the Holy Spirit. The same presence I felt when I saw the Lord in my room. I knew that this was another page in my life. I knew that this morning will be another morning I will be meeting with God. I felt everything around me went still; time froze as the glory of God came into my room. The glory of God brings everything to silence so that He could be heard. The warmth of God's presence felt like a blanket covering my being. Then I heard the voice of the Holy Spirit for the first time. It was the first time I heard the audible voice of the Holy Spirit. Perhaps I was too busy reading the Bible, or ignoring the contact He wanted to make. He spoke to me like a person would. My first thought was that it was someone outside calling me, maybe a friend of the family. It was loud and clear, with a tone that presents with authority. Although the voice was caring, it sounded warm and approachable.

I would never forget that morning because it was the first sermon I was preparing. It was a three point sermon from the book of Malachi. I could not believe how scriptures were popping into my thoughts and each one a valuable source of information for each point I was making. The sermon was being played before my eyes as a story, its vividness was as clear as the movies. Point after point I saw the illustration and the story as it related to the congregation. The potency of the information was stimulating. I saw the earth consumed in fire, but the fire was not affecting the saints of God. The saints of God were all dressed in white and were worshiping the Lamb of God. They were the ones who have been tested with fire while on the earth, the ones who were given fire by the Holy Spirit and it could do them no harm.

I reflected on the story of Shadrach, Meshach and Abednego with the Lord standing in the midst and not one hair of God's people was burnt. No one showed signs of concerns or disappointments, instead they all were more caught up in worshipping the Lord. People appeared as though they were waiting for this time to come and was relieved that it finally came. They were happy and grateful to God for their salvation. The glory of God formed a shield around the believers that the fire had no effect on them. Each transmitted faith and it ascended to the Father, and the anointing of the Holy Spirit kept everyone secured. The blood of Christ was their shield.

Upon completion of the sermon, I was overwhelmed; I could have written a book with the wealth of information given. It was new and fresh with rhema after rhema to take in. I offered a prayer to the Lord, "This is good, if it is for me I am grateful, however if it is for your people, ask or inspire the pastor to have me share this message this coming week." The message was too good to be just for me, besides I knew that it was another step to which I was being led. A preparation of developing boldness before crowds was necessary in my role as an evangelist.

Be careful what you ask for, God never forgets our prayer requests. That night I went to a men's meeting and surprisingly enough, the pastor asked if I could share "a word" at the Thursday night mid-week service. I knew I was being stretched and that it was another level I needed to climb. I knew that I needed to face my fear of speaking to crowds, getting out of my comfort zone. I was nervous, yet full of joy that it was my first sermon. I believe that the pastor had no clue as to what was going to happen, I however had a glimpse.

I came to the church early that Thursday night, met at the pastor's office and got all the wonderful words of advice. The elders prayed for the anointing to fall upon me, the pastor encouraged me to keep my focus on the message and to allow God to move through me. Then the hour came and I was called to minister the word. I was sitting at the front of the congregation with all the pastors and elders, and my eyes were on the crowd as it grew bigger and bigger. There was worship, testimonies, offerings, and then the time for a Word from the Lord. The pastor introduced me to the congregation, as I stood up; he embraced me and took his seat. On the platform stood a large wooden pulpit, which would become useful as a result of my fear. I was grateful that waist down my body was hidden cause my knees were shaking and I needed the support of the pulpit. Other less obvious signs were my mouth was quivering, my heart was pounding and my thoughts were racing.

I asked the congregation to join me in prayer as I looked to the Lord. I knew this too will pass and that it's another spurt of growth for me. As the voices soared to heaven, I had a private conversation with the Lord. I said "Lord, I cannot do this". It was becoming unbearable for me, my legs wanted to give way, and my lips were trembling like someone was pulling it with invisible strings. I keep assuring myself I will be okay, but to no avail. Again I said to the Lord, "I cannot do this". Then I heard the voice of the Holy Spirit saying, "Harrison, when you cannot do it, that's when I can do it through you". In this my strength was renewed. The sweetest words I ever heard. Up to this day, I have cherished those words. A peace came upon me, as I felt the arms of God over me. This momentous moment took place while the congregation was praying, as the prayer came to an end.

I realized everyone was staring at me. I knew that many people were disappointed that I was asked to deliver the sermon. The premise for this dissatisfaction was because many were committed much longer than I have been, and was never given the opportunity to address the congregation with the Word of God. Some were original participants at the onset when the church was planted and felt they were equipped to share, yet they were never asked to share the Word. I also think age was a factor as well, as I was only 17 years old at this time.

In the midst of beginning my sermon, I literally saw the sermon came out of the page as I began to give the Word. As the lesson came out of the pages in front of me, I began to speak with a bold assurance. I soon became confident as the message was being delivered. I was not even halfway through my sermon, when the power of God fell, and men and women began rushing up at the altar. It was my first sermon, and the first time I saw hungry people wanting prayer. They were kneeling at the altar, old and young. I could not believe what I was seeing. The Word of God was becoming stronger and stronger as the anointing drew the people to repentance and holiness.

As the Glory of God saturated the atmosphere, people were becoming filled with the Holy Spirit. Many were crying and weeping before the Lord. The whole atmosphere felt dense, a comforting feeling like a security blanket and it was pacifying those who were in need. God was making Himself known in a real way to everyone present. The meeting was filled with power, the kind of power that surpasses all earthy power that men seek after. Demons in several individuals began to be manifested. Hearts were surrendered to the Lord as the presence of the Holy Spirit swept through the room. Those at the altar remained there for over an hour. People were powerless to leave such a presence.

I was led to lay hands on those that came to the altar; the pastors proceeded to do the same. As I laid hands on those seeking prayers, most fell under the power of the Holy Spirit. This was all new to me; I thought God was pushing them down to break the power of fear over their lives. I did not know how this power affected people. The faith I had belonged to was void of power and I was not told of such happenings when I came to this faith, moreover even the seasoned members were taken by surprise which added to my already confused state. There were others on whom no one laid hands and they were falling over. All I can think of was that a higher and mightier force was affecting us and in His presence we were mere feeble human beings, unable to stand before this majestic presence.

The mood was like the day I was filled with the Holy Spirit. The energy level increases as the power was released. Mortals succumb to the presence of God. We are powerless in His sight. When we face this type of encounter the blue print for our life is reinforced and we persevere in fulfilling our destiny. In life we pursue a different course, one that the world cannot understand. This is exactly what this incident did to me. My coach was pushing me to yet higher limits. I was being presented with new challenges as doors of opportunity followed one after the other. I was called upon to speak at church meetings, public street meetings, crusades, tent meeting and parades. The more I yielded myself to the Holy Spirit, the more the doors opened. At 18 years old I was asked to take a pastoral role, however I declined for the simple reason that the Holy Spirit did not sanction it. The position did intimidate me, however if my coach wanted me to, the nervousness would of faded away, giving me the strength to hold fast even in adverse conditions.

WALK WITH ME

Growing up in a poor family has taught me frugality. I learnt how to survive from my parents. My father worked hard to earn a living and to maintain his family. We could not afford to indulge in what many took for granted. We applied thrift by cultivating a kitchen garden to its maximum. It supplied us with tomatoes, peas and a variety of other vegetables depending on the season. Ground provision also known as root vegetables were a mainstay. As much as possible transportation was on foot. The currency in use was not strong as our Canadian dollar. My weekly allowance was $20.00 (Trinidad and Tobago dollars) equivalent to approximately $3.20 Canadian dollars. Occasionally I would get an extra five dollars ($0.80 Canadian dollars). Local transportation to and from school was four dollars and a dollar would buy me a very basic snack. My wardrobe consisted of one pair trousers and two shirts.

My school was deep in the country, with sparse population, lots of farm land and uncultivated land graced my path between home and school. It took over ninety minutes walking one way without resting or stopping for a break. I walked most days in high school, except when the weather was bad. Occasionally I would hitch-hike with the trucks or school teachers early in the morning, nevertheless most evenings I took the solitary trail on foot. (Approximately one hour and thirty minutes on foot). As bad as it may seem, the time went by quickly as I walked home. During which time I was occupied in deep conversation with the Holy Spirit. Even if the conversation was one sided it was well spent.

He was my best friend, I knew He would never hurt me, speak badly about me, tease me, or bully me. He would never abuse or be insulting to me. He accepts and loves me for who I am, I did not have to impress Him. He indulged me with His heavenly tongue and I utilized every opportunity to participate with Him in this unknown tongue.

I was so absorbed with Him that I became oblivious to the heavy books in my bag, walking up and down hills, sometimes being rained on, or even being splashed on from trucks passing by. The roads were narrow and winding and vision was obscured by the trees on both sides of the unpaved road. All students wore uniforms, and each student could be identified as to which school they attended. Because of our uniforms, drivers were more inclined to offer us a ride since they felt safer with students rather than with the general public. Even strangers would stop to offer a ride; however I was taught never to ride with strangers.

There was one instance I decided to accept an offer from a few of my classmates. They asked for me to join them after school one Friday afternoon. I felt the need to be accepted by my peers so I took them up on their offer. The plan was for us to go for a ride up a limestone hill with a friend who drove a truck. All week the Holy Spirit was warning me against this decision. His message was telling me that this was not a friendly gesture; these boys had their own agenda. I kept on ignoring this message, I wanted to belong to this popular group and this was my opportunity. There was not the usual interaction between myself and the Holy Spirit that entire week. It seemed like I decided to turn the volume down. I did not want to listen to the promptings of Holy Spirit. I felt pressured internally as I was deliberately ignoring Him.

That Friday I went to school like any other school day. During my lunch break, I overheard one of the guys saying "We will make a fool of him". I knew they were talking about me as I was to be the new addition to the group. I ignored what I heard, I felt I could get them to like me, but then the Holy Spirit was persistent in speaking to me about being in danger. I could hear Him saying "walk with Me, come walk with Me".

The school bell rang for dismissal. The plan was to meet outside the gates by the entrance of the school. As I approached the gates, I kept on walking without stopping; I continued my walk until I reached home. The following week, I found out that the truck crashed that Friday because the driver was intoxicated. The five boys who had invited me to join them were seriously hurt and one almost died.

When I heard the news I was deeply touched with sorrow as I was brought to the realization how persistent the warning was and what could have happened to me if I had rebelled. I came to trust the Holy Spirit even more, appreciating His ability to know all things. He is the Alpha and the Omega, He is part of the Godhead, He is God's spirit, and is here to lead us into all truth. This incident pushed me closer, deepening my relationship with the Holy Spirit. I depended on Him as my coach. I surrendered to Him as an athlete preparing to be trained for the race. There was a clear determination in my heart to be someone in society who people will see in me a difference and through this relationship; they can see Him to be a real and a caring God.

MY COACH

THE MORE TIME I spent with the Holy Spirit, the more I realized that He is truly here to help me fulfil my purpose and destiny. We know He will lead, guide, instruct, counsel, teach, help and provide all the necessary support we may need to accomplish God's plan for our life. Walking with Him will increase our strength to push forward for more of God and less of self. During this time of my life, I recognized that I had to depend on the Holy Spirit to lead me in life. I knew that there would be no one who was willing to invest time to nurture me as He would, so He became my Coach.

I saw myself to be a spiritual athlete and the Holy Spirit to be my coach. Most coaches would agree that their goal is to provide the support and guide the athlete so he or she could attain the prize. That goal is keeping your eyes on the gold medal. With the Holy Spirit by your side the gold medal is an obtainable goal within reach. The secret is to submit to His authority. His focus is not to attain the bronze or the silver medallion; but the golden medallion. He wants only the best for us. The relationship between a coach and athlete evolves as time goes by; it is not something that happens over night. The coach should always be recognized as being in charge, the one who takes the authoritative role, much like parents to their child or a teacher to a student. As the child grows the relationship progresses until a point is reached and the bond matures into a meaningful partnership.

When I was in high school, I took on a role to support the coach. I could not comprehend the weight of the responsibility they had to carry. Their main concern was the safety of each player and within those parameters, to develop each athlete to his/her full potential. Trust and respect were two words which were foundational in establishing a meaningful relationship before the two could operate together as a team.

Unlike some coaches who may not have the experience or talent to work with some athletes, the Holy Spirit is not limited in His capability or specialization, He comes from the heart of God and is equipped and knows all things. There is no situation in life in which He cannot guide us with absolute authority, knowing that it is the best path. We have an advantage of allowing Him to train us to develop our full potential.

Respect and trust are two main criterions for a practical working relationship. It is the responsibility of a coach to ensure that his knowledge and experience are appropriate for the level and accomplishment of the athlete. We must realize that the Holy Spirit takes into account our level of experience and works with us to the next level. Our willingness to give of ourselves is the availability, then He uses whatever capability we have to accomplish the next task with the ultimate goal of giving the glory to God. We are just earthen vessels to be used to achieve or bring about the will of the Father.

Our availability is the guiding principle for the administration of His work. Without this accessibility our capability is useless to Him. We are still ready clay in the hands of the potter if we lack the capability (due to life's circumstances) but have the latent aptitude. In our race against time a believer is blest with the Holy Spirit who is willing to spend quality time with us whenever He is needed. His abiding presence to guide, counsel and teach is a priceless service to the child of God. When we are weak He is strong, His help is conditional. Depending on the freedom of access He is given to operate in our life, will determine the support we receive. As free agents we have the right to exercise choice, when this is done through worldly motive it will only prove a hindrance to our spiritual growth.

Having the Holy Spirit as our coach, we will learn to respect each other by recognizing the value in each other and the discernment of the work of the spirit in our lives. This is valuable in bringing people together for a greater work. Selfish motives will blind and limit His work. He works through others to encourage and strengthen our faith. Working as a team for one common goal is a force to be reckoned with.

We are mortals and are not equipped to work without getting tired and burnt out. Our bodies were not made to work without rest. The work of God needs others and though delegation we can rejuvenate. We all have to recognize our boundaries and the power that is working through us. When self gets the credit of the work done through us we are in the process of self destruction. The Spirit will leave us to our own demise. The failure of many in working together with others is the inability to accept who was sent in their path without judging, by appearance, charisma, past association by which the world determines as successful or even the threat as to who will get the glory for a job well done. His rules and values are in great contrast to man's, in fact the wisdom of man is foolishness in His eyes and in His work He confounds the wise.

THE RIGHT SETTING

AS MENTIONED EARLIER once we avail ourselves to the Holy Spirit, He will lead us and teach us in the right path. The teacher must familiarize him/herself with the student and his/her needs. The teacher then establishes a goal, and determines the method to be used to accomplish the set goals. Once the resolve between both teacher and student is inducted, lines of communication are open and both understand the expectations and accountability of each other. To teach is much more than the impartation of knowledge to the other. The individual has to be conditioned to a certain action or frame of mind before learning takes place. The instructor must set the mode to exude the ambience conducive to learning. Body language and lifestyle are also important factors in learning.

Every school we attend starting from kindergarten sets the crèche for learning. Our tools for learning were pencils, paper, art and craft supplies, the teacher's board and proper seating for the pupils. This formal setting gives us the cues that learning is to be taken seriously. The teacher projected an air of authority that sent the message that he/she is in control. There is a discipline to which we have to confirm until we are out of school.

Discipline is a life skill that takes us through life in our profession or in the workplace regardless of the type of work. When we consider the life of a pilot, our thoughts soar to airplanes, flying, altitude, maps, and someone trained to man the craft to its destination. A chauffeur, on the other hand leads us to envision a limousine, clean vehicle, rich and important people in positions of importance. While an officer would be someone in authority, who is familiar with the law of the land, weapons, the smell of substances. His authority supersedes the authority of the red light or speeding limit since his errand is a matter of life or death, peace or war. Yet we are to obey the law of the land and his job is to make sure the general public adhere to the law for the safety of others. He also knows the consequences to be applied for each infraction or to refer the person to a higher authority to deal with the situation in a court of law. The offender then pays the consequence for his action when judgement is passed.

Now what about Christians? What picture is projected at such a title? How many use this title without any regards as to discipline it entails. Our example of Christians is best seen in Jesus and His twelve disciples. These men were in total obedience to Jesus even though many times they did not fully grasp His mission. They followed with blind faith trusting in Him as the sheep trusting the shepherd. Today we think of Christians as pious individuals exhibiting Christian values by being caring, giving, generous, kind and showing love one to another. They can be approached for prayer; they are expected to know the word of God and are someone who can be depended upon.

The picture is an invention of the mind and does not apply in the majority of cases; the lifestyle of the individuals brings disgrace to this honourable tile. This title has been so blatantly misused, because we assign this name without realizing the full accountability involved. This dishonour to the image of Christ has caused those who think they know Him to trivialize their position in Him by riding on the waves of grace that He so generously endowed on man. There is no established principle to measure the standard of qualification of a Christian. If Christians were on trial for being a Christian, only a remnant would be found guilty as charged. This demonstrates the callous use of this entitlement with no regards to meet the required expectation.

There is a tendency for Christians to expect the working of the Holy Spirit in their lives, but here is where the rubber meets the road, man will continue to fool man but not the reader of hearts and the searcher of minds. If our identity as Christians if fruitless and unsound, the Holy Spirit cannot function under these pretentious conditions. He proves how genuine we are by our heart and our pledge of allegiance to seek God with all our heart mind and soul and to love our neighbour as ourselves. Through the Holy Spirit our identity is proven. As a coach, when progress is impeded the coach works with the athlete to overcome the obstacle that is hindering progress. The Holy Spirit does the same; we rely on Him to go before us and are assured because there is none like Him.

He became strong in my life; to the point where I became totally dependant on Him. I acknowledged Him as my coach, my comforter, my teacher, leader and instructor. My life was being transformed and those around me recognized my transformation. The secret was my dependency of the Holy Spirit. There was a price, I did not exert my free choice to follow my will but I surrendered myself to His divine will. The right setting is critical in order for the Holy Spirit to have His way. It is immanent to learn His way and follow His path. He sets the limitations and only when we can see through His eyes we are in the right place.

DEPENDENCY

WHEN SOMEONE BECOMES dependent on alcohol, drugs, gambling, smoking and other stimuli for pleasurable purpose, the person is considered to have an addiction. This is because the person has little or no control over the choice to kick the habit. As the use increases the more dependent the person becomes for the effects on him/her and they are considered to be in bondage to that habit. However there is never a place of respite instead the craving increases and so the individual needs it with more frequency or greater strength until they are utterly consumed by this vice. In like fashion we should depend on the Holy Spirit, craving Him more and more except the end is not a vice but victory.

On several occasions while at a family dinner, or out somewhere with others, the Holy Spirit prompted me to pray in fellowship. Like a smoker who escapes the crowd to take a puff for five to fifteen minutes, I have had to so such. We should be able to do the same in answer to this call of duty. Someone's life may be in the balance between life and death where our intercession is needed while there is still life. We may be called to intercede for someone who may be in impending danger and prayer is needed. Sometimes it is just getting prepared to speak to someone where it takes only the supernatural power of the Holy Spirit to break the walls around their life. The Holy Spirit may use it as a message, a prophetic message, a word of wisdom or a warning. The conversation may be getting off key and He wants to assure you that He is by your side. It is important we grasp every opportunity to keep Him close.

People around you will be affected either in a positive or negative way. Remember everywhere Jesus went while He was on this earth, people were affected by His presence. He carried the power of the Holy Spirit with Him. Some wanted to get closer to Him, others wanted to kill him. Why should it be different for the believer? The same Spirit which moved on the face of the deep from creation is the same Holy Spirit who raised Christ from the dead and He dwells in you and me. The power source of heaven lives in us. We have so much to learn about utilizing His power within us.

As a teenage before moving to Canada, my parents were able to take the entire family for dinner at least once a month. Even though it was only at a KFC restaurant my siblings and I appreciated what our parents did. But there were times where total strangers came up to where we were seated and would begin swearing and speaking gibberish. This bothered me for years; I could not understand why this happened to us, why did he not address others? It was as if we did something to him. It embarrassed us especially my younger siblings. My mom would console us by saying that they were crazy people. On one occasion, as we were being accosted, I said "devil I rebuke you". To this day I am not sure if the person heard me, or if anyone else heard me, nevertheless the person stopped in his tracks and went through the doors. Later the Holy Spirit revealed to me that those people were reacting to the presence of God in us because they were possessed by demons.

I now understood that as we walk with the Lord and are drawn closer to Him, His presence is recognized and others can be troubled by His light. Light always dispels darkness and those who resist react in a negative way. The Holy Spirit works in partnership with us, and without Him we are like dry bones, like Christians who may have a lot of head knowledge and life experience but no power. When we become dependent on the Holy Spirit, our life changes, the Holy Spirit takes all our knowledge and experience and uses them as lessons in life. They become our testimony and it touches more hearts as the Holy Spirit brings it to light. He is the essence of life; he who knows Him can no longer live without Him.

Dependency

I had attended a service where the presence of God was quite evident. There I ministered the Word of God; the theme was about the glory of God. The power of the Holy Spirit filled the sanctuary, and the altar crowded with souls needing a touch from God. It was a service focused on healing in that I would pray for people and believe God for their healing. In the midst of these healing prayers as I laid hands on one of the attendees, I was caught up in a vision. I saw myself at the bottom of a high wall. I was praying, but I felt that nothing was happening as the wall appeared to be thick and high, built with huge stones and massive rocks. I did not relent in my prayers because it was a prayer of expectation, even though I had no clue as what to expect. I thought maybe the walls represented a barrier for the person and maybe it will crumble and the person will receive a blessing.

To my surprise a most unlikely thing happened. In my prayers the Holy Spirit came in the form of a person by my side and said "you can use my shoulders to stand upon in order to see what's on the other side", assuring me that He will be my support as long as I trust in Him as my strong tower. The view was to prepare me for what was involved in praying for others and the different forms of obstacles operating in people's lives. The scene before me was a wide gamut of garbage in the lives of people. These barriers were a hindrance as to why so many who are prayed for do not receive from the Lord.

Of the myriad reasons before me this particular case on hand was unique. I saw this person's hurdle as various colours of cords representing the many decisions and choices facing him, combined with his viewpoint in life. It created an enormous blockage from receiving. Man tends to depend on his own strength only to realize in the end he is powerless and all strength comes from God. Oh yes, for a while we live in a fantasy world crediting our accomplishments to self, until the crossroad of life awakens us as to who is in charge. Fortunately some come to their senses early in life to recognize the source of their strength.

God our creator knows us by name and number; He is acquainted with every fibre of our being, every hair on our head. When He made man He said "It is good", so He wants good things for His people. He wants to bless His people, to be their God and for them to enjoy His blessing. The ego is a contradiction to God, the ego credits self for every achievement and success in life, and it hungers after money, power and control. There is no real peace and joy of living. If only they understood that the key to success is to trust in Him to carry us.

Ever since that vision, I have learnt to be aware of the deterrents that constrains the work of the Holy Spirit because He does not have full access to work in us with these limitations. The lesson I have learnt is that to keep the power of God alive, I need to trust and obey God. I need to cultivate habits that will discharge any garbage, to relinquish self and instead become dependent on the Holy Spirit when I minister the Word of God.

Even though many men of God understand this principle yet as we mature in our Christian walk we fall when we lean on our own understanding. We sometimes forget that the arms of flesh will fail; of course many times this takes place at the subconscious level. Some relive their experiences of what it used to be when the Holy Spirit was functioning in their lives. However without the presence of the Holy Spirit, we could only operate in the flesh. We have to live in constant expectation because the Spirit of God is always around; His purpose is not for works but to build faith. Therefore the experiences are good, when it reminds people of how God operates and will continue to do so in ways that will confound man. As we grow with the Holy Spirit, the greater our experiences will become. Our maturity with Him flows with power. Our life portrays God's presence and character.

DISPEL THIS FEAR

EVEN THOUGH I was still young my past experiences have taught me that the Holy Spirit takes every opportunity to open doors for the Word of God to go forth. Since I was first filled with the Holy Spirit, it created a desire in me to pray, to earnestly seek the face of God, to delve into His Word and to expound on His truth. My determination to open the doors of opportunity to avail myself by Him in any way He sees fit, I am the willing vessel.

My first visit to Canada was in April, 1986. The Canadian way of life was quite new to me yet I continued evangelizing, preaching and teaching the Word of God. I would go to the busy street corners where I lived to share about Jesus with the youths. Some of the youths referred to me as "Moses" who had a new drug called "Jesus". I truly believe the Holy Spirit's desire is to bring people to the knowledge of Christ and I was committed, I would not let anything deter me from this mission. If He is willing to work with anyone who is willing to avail themselves why should I expect someone else to do the job? When I need His Word He brings back into remembrance the scriptures I have studied. These scriptures are our ammunition; it's the sword we wield against the power of darkness, in our effort to advance the kingdom of God.

The third Friday of every month, I use to take a group of youths to Hamilton, Ontario to evangelize on the streets. Those who were willing to hear the gospel met at a "coffee house' where they were treated to a cup of coffee and a donut. They would take time to listen to the Word of God. They were also encouraged to visit the local church in their area. We would acquire permits to have public praise and worship, as well as Christian public speaking in downtown Hamilton.

On one such outing, I met two young girls who looked me straight in the eyes and said, "Satan is Lord". They said this with a passion. I felt like they actually believed what they were saying. These two girls were dressed in black, wearing black lipstick and their fingernails were covered with black nail polish. Their eyelids were heavily painted with black eye liner. They certainly were not dressed in the conventional female attire or were there any attempt in their dress to attract the opposite sex. It was obvious they belonged to some dark cult. Their intent was to discourage or disrupt our meeting. In all my years of evangelizing this was my first encounter with someone who actually believed in Satan. Both of them looked me in the eyes and said, "We will send Satan to your home tonight", after those words, fear came upon me. This sense of fear left me very uncomfortable so I asked my sister-in-law, who was with me, to pray with me to dispel this fear. Although the Holy Spirit gave me words to say and seeds of faith were planted in me, these words still haunted me.

That night at around midnight, I came down to our living room, waiting for the devil to show up. Somehow I did expect him to show up, and then I remembered our prayers for our home and family. We have always prayed for a hedge of protection around our home 50 feet around, above and beneath with the blood of Jesus. The Holy Spirit reminded me that our world is a spiritual world, and there are constant battles for our lives. The prayers we utter in faith create building blocks using Jesus' blood as the mortar to seal every crack to keep the walls strong.

Since then I never saw those girls again; however we kept them in prayer that the Lord will draw them to Himself. This was my first experience of witnessing faith being released on something one believes. They actually had believed in Satan and for them he was real.

Not much longer after this incident, the Holy Spirit showed me a picture of a football field, a massive football field. This field had a starting line and a finish line; however at the end of the finish line, I saw gifts being handed out to those who completed the entire track as the finishing line ended at the throne of God. I saw many people I knew who became weary and tired and were resting on the side. Some were busy chatting with others and did not appear to be interested in finishing. Then there were those who were aggressive and pushing others around as they were getting behind. Others were focused and on track. I saw where my life was and I knew that I needed to keep focused, otherwise I could be defeated or distracted from the plan, purpose and destiny God had designed for my life.

As I stayed in constant relationship with the Holy Spirit, I saw His anointing increase. The door to explore the power of God began flowing through the Holy Spirit. He took me into the throne of the Father and showed me the blood of Christ on the mercy seat crying mercy. Here is the key where quality multiplies. As the ministry is pursued with purity of mind, growth will follow as the day follows night. God will never forsake the righteous in His work.

GIFTS

THE HOLY SPIRIT is equipped with everything we need to authenticate the reality of God. He is looking for a relationship with only those trustworthy of His friendship. He will only use individuals who are willing to be vessels through whom He can work with. His work is done through the gifts of the Spirit. Qualified individuals would already be exhibiting qualities recognized as the fruit of the Spirit. Once this identification of credentials is in place and the person is in pursuit to fulfil his/her destiny, the Holy Spirit will distribute as He sees fit and according to the call. It is not for us to dictate to Him what we require, because He knows our needs. He will then coach us in handling His gifts. Through His wisdom these gifts will win souls into the kingdom of God and in so doing they are honouring God. The gifts are not ours but work though us. We take no credit for them since they are for the Glory of God.

I remember when I was courting my wife, not only did I want to see her every day, but I bought her gifts and flowers every time I came to see her. Her mother once remarked, "My house has become a flower shop". When we are in love it is our nature to give to those we love. Many of us can remember when we were young, our first week at school. Everyone was new to each other and there was no familiar face, no one to talk to. The first step is to talk to someone, once that happens the relationship develops where every day you spend more time together, eventually you may start sharing lunch, snacks and other foods. Then birthdays come along where you would give a gift.

As we get older so does the type of gifts, more suited for the age and ability of the recipient. Sometimes the form of gifts vary, more that pretty packages for personal use instead it is shared, perhaps going to a show together or spending time in each other's company by going for coffee or a meal. Even though the forms vary, a need is met where bonds strengthen. One of my wife's close friends, with whom she went to school, once took us to a clothing store and said, "choose whatever you want, the tab is on me". It was our first experience at such generosity and the joy of feeling special never left us.

If our earthly friends can go out of their way to make us feel special with gifts, how much more will the Holy Spirit. Unlike our friends, from whom we receive material things that will not stand the test of time or outlives its usefulness, the Holy Spirit give gifts that are priceless. These gifts men crave but they cannot be bought with material possessions. There are several gifts the Holy Spirit has in His possession which He wants to give to those He deems worthy of receiving or capable of handling, however there is a time and purpose in receiving these giftings. Our divine benefactor though generous, also applies wisdom in the distribution of these gifts. This is so they will compliment each other, working together as a whole in unity.

The Holy Spirit gives wisdom for those who function in leadership and administrative roles. The Bible tells us that Joseph was recognized by Pharaoh as possessing more than human attainments (Gen 41:38-40). There are many others recognized for having wisdom that was above the norm such as Joshua (Numbers. 27:18), Othniel (Judges. 3:9), Gideon (Judges. 6:34), Jephthah (Judges. 11:29), Saul (1 Samuel 10:10), David (1 Samuel. 16:13) and the list goes on.

In the Old Testament, there was the gift of special skills, those who were blessed with it excelled at that skill. The tailors were given special skills to sew the priestly garments (Ex. 28:3). All the necessary details and patterns needed as the blue print was given from God. We see the workmen for the tabernacle (Ex. 31:3, 35:30-35), who had an aptitude for that trade like Hiram of Tyre (1 King. 7:14).

The Holy Spirit gave people unusual physical strength. Most of us know the story of Samson (Judges. 13:25, 14:6,19 &15:14). We are familiar with the cause of his demise, the reason he lost his strength by taking for granted that which was endowed upon him. We will not be able to manifest the power of these gifts when we live in sin.

The gifts of miracles are also given to those who are marked by God. We see individuals like Moses, Elijah, Elisha, and Christ, the early apostles, and many revivalists and reformists today who operate in this gift. Jesus made it clear that the miracles were done by the power of the Holy Spirit (Matt 12:28). The gift is so unique; we need to make sure that it is not confused with natural or medical science, modern surgical skills, or anything associated with man's knowledge. It is a supernatural gift. God has always used miracles throughout the ages to increase the faith level of His people and to bring hope to a dying world. The apostle Paul revealed to the church, that the Holy Spirit distributes gifts to edify and build the body of Christ (1 Cor. 12:1-11). Paul identifies 9 gifts: Diversity of tongues, Word of Knowledge, Gifts of Healing, and Interpretation of Tongues, Word of Wisdom, Working of Miracles, Gifts of Prophecy, Discerning of Spirits, and Gift of Faith. Each one has its unique purpose.

Paul taught about the Five-Fold Ministerial Gifts (Ephesians 4:11). As we study the Word, we learn that each gift had a role and responsibility. Each was identified by its titles, such as Apostles, the Prophets, the Evangelists, the Pastors, and Teachers. In Romans 12:6-8, we learn of the Seven Motivational Gifts; Prophecy, Serving, Teaching, Exhortation, Giving, Ruling, and Mercy. All of these were given to build and edify the church and they should be recognized in the body of Christ. Some churches may not have these functioning, as the Holy Spirit has not found anyone in that congregation to give these gifts to, or the individuals are not being encouraged to develop these gifts.

In my childhood years my parents' economic situation did not permit us to have many gifts for birthdays and Christmas. When we did receive a gift it was usually simple and many times it was an old item re-wrapped to create excitement. During the Christmas holidays, my sister and I would wrap empty boxes, hoping that they will be filled. We would have a Christmas tree with lots of empty gift boxes. The wrappings were nothing fancy, just wrappings from the grocer or the daily newspaper. We used our worn socks to hang as stockings with match boxes wrapped up as gifts. The one gift I do recall receiving from my godfather was a train set. Anyway, there is a responsibility to the gifts we receive. After playing with it they must be cared for and put away properly. When the gift you are given is unfamiliar to you, training is necessary before you can make use of it. The Spirit coaches us in a like manner with the use of the gifts bestowed on us.

FRUIT

A PREREQUISITE TO receiving Spiritual Gifts is the fruit of the spirit. "Fruit of the Spirit" is a biblical term that sums up the nine visible attributes of a true Christian. These attributes are: love, joy, peace, longsuffering, gentleness, goodness, faith, meekness and temperance. (Galatians 5:22, 23,). We learn from scripture that these are not individual "fruits" from which we pick and choose. Rather, the fruit of the Spirit is one ninefold "fruit" that characterizes all who truly walk in the Holy Spirit. Collectively, these are the fruits that all Christians should be producing in their new lives with Jesus Christ.

Before looking at the 9 features of the fruit of the Spirit we must first understand the means of obtaining them. Christians should know that the fruit of the spirit are nine in total. The difference between the fruit of the Holy Spirit and the gifts of the Holy Spirit is in how they are obtained. The gifts are given while the fruit is earned. Gifts are given following the baptism in the Holy Spirit (Acts 19:6). So once we are sealed by the Holy Spirit, He will give gifts according to our strengths and capability. The gifts will only be given to us when the character of God through the fruit of the spirit starts developing. A rounded Christian displays the nine characters of the fruit of the spirit to a varying degree, thriving each day towards perfection. In so doing we develop the character of God within us and we project His image.

Having a background of a gardener, I learned that there is a season for planting and a season for harvesting. I learned that I cannot reap what I did not sow. Once a seed is planted, it needs to be taken care of like a child, making sure it is watered and has the proper sunlight. Like the fruit of the Holy Spirit, we ought to make sure we are constantly working on each flavour. The more time spent on nurturing the fruit, the greater we will be rewarded, both from God and people around us. It takes time and effort to produce the fruit of the Holy Spirit, no other alternative.

The Holy Spirit waits patiently for the fruit and gifts to work together. This is the perfect will of God as we reflect His character. He starts with giving everyone the fruit with all 9 flavours, and through prayer, communion, fellowship, and reading God's Word, these are developed. Once we are able to reflect God's character, the Holy Spirit will give gifts suitable to the individual according to the call and purpose. The fruit reflects the gifts and the gifts reflect the fruit. They both work hand in hand as they are of the Spirit and not of ourselves. The fruit will create the power of the Spirit to grow upon us like a wind, He will become stronger and carry us a long way in life.

WIND

I ENJOYED GROWING up on the island as a youth. One of my favorite times was the high wind season, as there was so much to do especially flying kites. I also enjoyed climbing trees and feeling the breeze blowing and moving the branches. At times I felt that I could fly away. I actually had many dreams of myself flying in the wind. The trees were always dancing with the wind, green and luscious.

I remembered in the 1970's there was a hurricane, where hundreds of people died including a friend who was in my class. He and his twin brother were in my class, and as a result of the hurricane, one wall fell and crushed him. He was taken to emergency, however never survived.

The hurricane came during school hours. We were sent home early, so I went by my grandmother who lived about five minutes away. The rain was pouring down and the wind was blowing. As the day went by, the weather grew worse with thunder and lightening flashing continuously. My grandmother held me, my cousin and my uncle close together on the main level of her home. The water was flooding into her main floor and we could see debris blowing all over and around the house as the wind carried it away. The rooftops were being blown away; pieces of homes were seen flying in the wind. People were screaming as their animals were being killed, or their homes were being blown to pieces.

I remembered looking out and seeing the trees moving in all directions from the power of the wind. No one could see the wind; however they could see the power of what it could do.

I became fascinated by wind. It is so strong that is cannot be defeated, flies faster than any moving objects or animal. It can go in whatever direction it chooses and no one can stop it. The wind can become a threat to life as it can cause damages. I soon learned about the different types of wind and what they can do. When the place is humid and it appears that there is no movement, this can be described as calm wind. It is flat and does nothing.

I like to think of the Holy Spirit as the wind. There were some services we attended where there was a light air. There is nothing to talk about, there may be a ripple here and there, but we cannot feel the presence of the Holy Spirit. We feel that the meeting is dry. Then there are services where one or two people are moved by the power of God. It feels like a 'light breeze'. It becomes visual like seeing some movement on leaves or bushes. Then we may witness a 'gentle breeze' where we can see more movements of the Holy Spirit. One can notice a constant move on a few individuals. The momentum grows as we see more and more people being touched. This can be described as a 'moderate breeze'.

On the island, many would say "there is a fresh breeze blowing". This is said when smaller trees sway. When the Holy Spirit begins to move, everyone will have a taste of His presence. Then like a 'strong breeze' the entire local church will witness the presence of God. Like looking at the ocean, there would be large waves, or large branches blowing. Everyone would be able to witness the move of the Holy Spirit. It does not stop here; the power of the Holy Spirit can be developed into 'a storm', where it becomes national. The entire country will hear about what He is doing. There will be signs, wonders and miracles. A revival will occur. Then something big arrives, the 'hurricane', when the entire world will become aware of the move of God. This is where everyone who comes into the presence of the Holy Spirit will be touched. Skeptic or not, the power of God will transform lives.

The wind may not seem like anything, however we can look right through it, and we can walk right through it. When there is a storm, it makes its presence known. Wind is able to lift roofs off buildings, blow down power lines and trees, and cause accidents.

When we see what the power of the wind can do, we can only imagine what the power of the Holy Spirit can do. He has been working from the beginning of time and have never ceased. The Holy Spirit's power is untouchable and no power in this world or the world to come can defeat Him. Every principality and power submits to His power. He was the same power that moved upon the face of the deep before the world began. He is the power which raised Christ from the dead. He is that power which moved on the day of Pentecost, the power that inspired men to write the Word of God and the power that is here to lead, guide and instruct. He is the Holy Spirit. Having said so, as much as He can be powerful like the wind, He can also take on the form of fire which is also another powerful force. In fact the Bible made it clear that we will be baptized with the Holy Spirit and with fire. What does this mean?

FIRE

"I indeed baptize you with water unto repentance: but he that cometh after me is mightier than I, whose shoes I am not worthy to bear: he shall baptize you with the Holy Ghost, and [with] fire" **Matthew 3:11**

WHEN WE THINK of fire, we think of a flames burning, emitting light as it burns. Flames are not the only evidence of fire. Fire and its potential are contained in sparks and smolders as in a cigarette butt. The flames we see are the end result of a chain reaction in the environment. Fire is ignited through the release of energy, usually friction or some flammable substances; it thrives on organic matter and needs oxygen to sustain it. At creation God created the sun that supplies man with heat and light. God has instilled man with the wisdom and propensity to use fire creatively.

Many of man's everyday needs were fulfilled by using fire. Man's penchant for comfort was the drive in finding many uses for fire. Mankind's greatest achievement is his ability to control fire in a portable form. Through this expertise man was able to generate heat and light, making it possible for people to migrate to colder climates, to sustain health which is a key step in the prevention of diseases through properly cooked foods. Other uses involve protection against wild animals, in forging tools, baking bricks for buildings and pottery for cooking utensils, and a host of others uses. Careless use when unchecked can have devastating results, destroying forests, wildlife, cities and human life.

God supplied the children of Israel with a pillar of fire at night to keep them warm on their journey from Egypt. Ancient Greeks considered fire one of the major elements in the universe, alongside earth, water, and air. Unlike earth, water and air, fire transforms the product it consumes, releasing and converting the form of energy into another totally unlike the original. It is also used to cleanse and burn out impurities on metals leaving it in a pure state. The spiritual facet of fire is not to meet our physical needs. The burning bush was not to warm Moses but to invigorate him and set him on a new path of life. The tongues of fire were not for the comfort of the disciples, rather it was to revitalize and regenerate the early church.

The word of God has the same effect as metal in fire. As on the metal the Word of God discharges an energy that changes us into purer beings. The Holy Spirit also makes His presence known as fire to sanctify man to make him pure before God; sin is the impurities like the dross in the metal. We need the Holy Spirit every day in our life to make life full and productive as we grow in the Lord. This fire of the Holy Spirit gives off more energy during prayer and fasting. The spark is always in the believer and is waiting to be ignited through prayer and fasting.

The environment has to be right; the need for the resurrection power of Jesus to be propagated must be the primary cause so that God may be glorified. The Holy Spirit will use human vessels to perform signs and wonders to transmit this message by dispelling darkness with its light by converting souls and bringing change as metal in the flame. Only through the Word of God will the Holy Spirit operate, no opinion, philosophy or doctrine will move Him. The fire of the Holy Spirit will keep on burning as long as we fuel the fire with the Word of God, prayer and fellowship. The larger the flame is, the stronger the heat. When we restrain the fire, within it cannot spread. Fire will only spread when it is not contained and the stronger the heat the greater the impact will be on others in transforming lives to the glory of God. Just like the Holy Spirit He leaves His mark when we are baptized in fire.

> *"I indeed baptize you with water unto repentance: but he that cometh after me is mightier than I, whose shoes I am not worthy to bear: he shall baptize you with the Holy Ghost, and [with] fire"* Matthew 3:11

Fire can destroy all of our possessions; it can reduce an entire forest to a pile of ash and charred wood. It's also a terrifying weapon, with nearly unlimited destructive power. It is used as a protection to keep our spiritual man pure and holy before God. It can burn all unwanted elements in our lives. The fire of the Holy Spirit can destroy the works of the devil and set many people free from the bondage of the devil.

What is the Role of Fire?

Fire is part of nature's cycle of renewal and re-growth. It is similar to droughts, floods, storms, and other natural disturbances that have quick and direct impact on people, plants and animals. Likewise the fire of the Holy Spirit has impacted our spiritual world from the beginning of time. When we think of a forest with all its plants at various stages of their life cycle, we can think of our spiritual world with all the different growth in the lives of Christians. Throughout the age, fire has been used to purge and to create new life. The Holy Spirit has been doing the same in the spiritual world. He has been using its creative power on those who avail themselves. As much as forest fires are natural, the Holy Spirit's fire is natural to those who have been born again. A forest fire occurs from lightning and natural sparks in the absence of human activity. The Holy Spirit will start a fire from a spark germinated from the Word of God, especially in those who are very dry.

As much as a natural fire can disrupt lives and communities, the Holy Spirit can do the same when revival is present. He can move like a fire and touch hundreds and thousands of lives, bringing them to the realization of the cross and the blood of Christ shed for their souls. When a natural fire is present, everyone becomes aware of it and cannot deny that it exists. Some may try to contain it and put it out, however those around will know. When the Holy Spirit is present, the entire world should know about it and how His presence is touching lives. There will be no second guessing as to what is working in the lives of men and women; no one will be able to doubt in His existence. The contagious effect on others infected through the testimonies and changed lives is what it takes to set the world on fire.

Fire is known by its size and intensity. Like a snow flake, no two fires are the same. When the Holy Spirit moves He moves as He sees fit. He will make Himself known that all will see the power in the cross. He is never with us to glorify Himself, but to glorify Christ. His presence is here to get the attention of the world, and is looking for anyone who will avail themselves.

We have seen how small fires are easy to control. We can see how this could apply to small groups. If the leader is not spirit-filled, he or she will not inflame others but rather dampen any spark there is since the spirit is subject to the prophet. Leadership is usually afraid that a small fire can cause serious injuries and damages, so they quench the Holy Spirit before He can move. The moment some leaders smell smoke, they look for all means possible to prevent the Holy Spirit from moving, especially if the Holy Spirit is not moving within their program. We need to understand that we cannot put God in a box and need to allow the Holy Spirit the freedom to move as He wills.

Many protestant churches have removed the use of oil from the altar. Oil symbolizes fuel that kindles fire. As expressed in the Bible, oil is used for anointing. The Holy Spirit has been marginalized by the limitations we impose on His work. Our anointing is effective when we lay hands on the sick. Why limit this activity when sometimes the sick may need to be anointed with oil, and this may be the avenue required for this situation. We don't call the shots on how the Holy Spirit should operate; He needs free reign to accomplish His duties. There are various forms designated for the transfer of power in the execution of signs and wonders. This has been clearly demonstrated in both the old and new testament. The oil may be the healing balm for that malady or sickness. The scriptures tell us:

> *"Is any among you sick? Let him call for the elders of the church, and let them pray over him, anointing him with oil in the name of the Lord, and the Lord will raise him up."* James 5:14

HARRISON S. MUNGAL

The Holy Spirit desires to administer our lives in a way that is most appropriate to Him; He craves to become involved and yearns to glorify God. He is not looking for golden or silver vessels, He is looking for men and women who will learn how to yield themselves and become available. The Holy Spirit desires to become our friend and coach.

FRIENDSHIP

"I DON'T HAVE any friends" one of my daughters said to me after her first day of school. With tears streaming down her cheeks, she went on to say, "But dad I have Jesus who is my friend". We all should have friends. There are touching poems and stories of friendships. No man is in island, men are social beings and it is their human nature to crave friends. Some may substitute animals as companions and friends, but this is never an adequate alternative. Animals may bring joy but communication is limited, some get satisfaction by surrounding themselves with nature or even works of art, nevertheless only another human can share in the passion of these interests.

Everyone needs and longs for a true friend. In the past, deterrent factors such as a lack of trust, betrayal, or ingratitude may contribute to this adverse preference. Deep down this inherent need is being suppressed. Shame is another restriction in opening up to others, and past hurt from a loved one has left scars that need to be healed. True friends are rare and hard to find, however if you never venture you can never gain. Life includes risks, family and acquaintances are stepping stones in developing relationships and friendships; yet in a true friend one could receive advice, inspiration and support.

Time is an essential element in procuring a friend, a friend can handle your talents and your weaknesses and accept you for who you are, whose motive is pure and is always willing to forgive. Friendship entails loyalty, respect, sincerity, trust, love, reliability, openness, honesty, companionship and accountability. There must be a freedom to share likes and dislikes, interests, differences and similarities. There should never be a fear of feeling that one would be judged or criticized in a negative way.

A classical example in the Bible is God to Abraham, Abraham had developed a relationship with God (Genesis 18:17-33). God said "Shall I hide from Abraham what

I am doing". Abraham responded by telling God his thoughts and feelings about the situation. This could have only been possible because of their mutual relationship. From this faith and trust, Abraham was promised to be the father of many nations, and that his seeds would be like the sand on the sea. Abraham paid a price to earn this type of friendship, and it was worth it. God and Abraham were able to do this because there was trust and respect between each other.

Another example of true friends was that of David and Jonathan found in first Samuel 20. They cared for each other and had great trust and confidence in one another. The friendship started after David's duel with Goliath and was reported to Jonathan's father, King Saul. "Jonathan became one in spirit with David and he loved him as himself" (1 Samuel 18:1). When Jonathan saw David, he felt a soul connection with him. "He loved him as himself." They had a lot in common; both were warriors being commendable and courageous men. Jonathan "smote the Philistine outpost at Geba" (1 Samuel 13:3), and became a hero. Jonathan made a covenant with David by the exchange of garments. He took off the robe he was wearing and gave it to David, along with his tunic, and even his sword, his bow and his belt" (18:2-4). This was a covenant of commitment to friendship for life, it was initiated by Jonathan, binding himself to love David, and sealing the covenant with the gift of his armor. He gave David his armor, which was his means of defense. David on the other hand had nothing to give.

Another example was between Christ and Peter (John 18). Although Peter would deny his friend and Saviour, he was forgiven (John 21).

Christ love for humanity is the greatest example from which one can learn, someone who was willing to lay down His life for His friends (John 15). The Bible states that a friend is one who sticks closer than a brother (Proverbs 18:24).

We should always be supportive to our friends. We display friendship to God when we can express this relationship with another human being.

Looking around and observing people in relationships, I saw a great need for true friendships in the lives of those around me. After an understanding of what should take place among individuals I detected a sad lack on both sides. When we have an understanding of what our Lord commanded "to love your neighbour as yourself" then we would grasp the full importance of this great commandment. When we do unto others as we would have them do to us we become accountable for our actions. We foster a relationship with the Holy Spirit and we are encouraged by His presence and enjoy every moment with Him. We have an understanding of trust and respect. We become dependable and reliable as He gives His love unconditionally. Unlike man, the Holy Spirit cannot deny Himself (2 Tim. 2:13). He cannot lie (Titus1:2, Heb. 6:18), He cannot tempt man neither can He be tempted to sin (James 1:13), He cannot do things absurd or self-contradictory nor can he have favour over iniquity (Heb. 1:13)

When we look at the relationship with Christ and the Holy Spirit, we see that the Holy Spirit was with Him from His conception (Matt. 1:8, 20-21; Lk. 1:35). Jesus was born of and filled with the Holy Spirit from the moment of conception (Isa. 11:2-3, 42:1-4; 61:1-2, Lk. 4:1; Luke 1:15; Jn 3:34). We learn that Christ was led by the Holy Spirit while He was on the earth (Matt. 4:1). He was able to cast out devils (Matt 12:28), Jesus gave man the promise of His constant companion (Acts 1:5), performed miracles (Matt. 12:28; Lk. 11:20, 4:14-15,18, Isa. 61:1-2.), baptized, gave spiritual gifts, the list goes on and on. The miracles of Christ were performed in the power of the Holy Spirit (Mk. 5:30; Lk. 8:46, Lk. 5:17, 6:19). When Christ was alone in the wilderness (Mk. 1:12) the Holy Spirit was present. He was there at the resurrection (Acts 2:24, Jn 11:25, Eph. 1:17-20, Jn 11:25, 10:17-18, Romans 8:11, 1 Peter 3:18, Rom. 1:4).

Christ was never alone while He was walking on this earth. His life was an example for us, when He departed He left the Holy Spirit to have the same relationship with us as with Him. The Holy Spirit is seeking human vessels to live in and to demonstrate His power through us so we may magnify God.

The Holy Spirit wants to flow in His role as a friend to the Church. He wants to regenerate (Jn 3:5; Titus 3:5). His desire is to give dreams and visions like He did through the prophets, kings, priests, Jesus, and the early church. God wants to make Himself known through the Holy Spirit. He gave men the inspiration to write the Word and to enlighten us as to His ways. From the illumination of His Word, man receives revelation and wisdom to guide him. The elucidation received from the Word to the heart of man is not because of mans ability but the work of the Holy Spirit in him. He brings convictions and sanctifies us with the Word, reminding us that there is forgiveness in Christ. He intercedes on our behalf and guides us into all truth. He builds us up in faith every time we receive a surge of His power. We can build ourselves in faith when we pray in the Holy Spirit. (Jude 20).

There never was a better friend than the Holy Spirit. He knows our every need and He is always timely with His help. Man's impatience has been our downfall. Our lack of sight and our feelings of self importance can cloud our vision to the work of God. Every situation in life is a lesson for ministry, as our endurance is strengthened through them. Besides, our mandate is to conform to the perfect will of God. In retrospect we see the big picture and we get a glimpse of how the God meets our every need. If we trust him and know the lines of communication are always open to His children, why should we worry, did He not say we have no power of making one hair white or black? Where is our trust? He has given us the assurance of our value to Him by comparing us to the little sparrow.

Friendship with the Holy Spirit does not develop overnight, we toil daily pursuing spiritual ideals in life. We have to shadow Him. This means we have to be acquainted with His ways, with His likes and dislikes, His character and His abilities. We come to the point of a union by developing a 'like-mindedness' with Him.

I still remember the days as a new Christian. As I was on my way to church I was prepared as to what hymns will be sung, and the lesson for the congregation. He would also guide me as to whom I would meet, and whether or not I will be invited to speak. To this day I still depend on this intuition prompted by the Holy Spirit.

HARRISON S. MUNGAL

The prayer of David "take not thy Holy Spirit from me" reveals the heart of a man who understood how to fellowship with the Holy Spirit, sin can affect this rapport; man's affiliation with the Holy Spirit is a precious bond. I can relate to David as these words resound in my heart for I know not how I could exist without Him. To think of the darkness without Him is incentive enough to stay in His light. This is one of the main reasons I love to evangelize. Bringing a lost soul from darkness into the marvelous light incites me to do battle against the forces of darkness.

When a newly converted believer is walking in the light he is conscious of the stumbling blocks in his path. His dependence on the Holy Spirit to coach him through these obstacles as he surrenders to the Lord truly brings glory to God. However all do not show the same strength to refrain from their past, so like babes they stumble as they grope towards the light. The Holy Spirit will not depart from them in their time of need. He desires to change that. He wants the world to see that we are co partners with Him. He wants the world to see that He has been coaching us and training us to be the best we can be and He longs for us to bring glory to Christ. He moves in us with signs and wonders according to the promise made by Christ.

SIGNS AND SYMBOLS

"And these signs shall follow them that believe; In my name shall they cast out devils; they shall speak with new tongues; They shall take up serpents; and if they drink any deadly thing, it shall not hurt them; they shall lay hands on the sick, and they shall recover." Mark 16:17,18

SIGNS AND SYMBOLS are a language in that which it communicates a message. There are various forms of signs and symbols. A sign may say one thing clearly, without ambiguity. A stop sign at an intersection is decisive in its meaning. A sign is the most direct way of communication, unlike a symbol that represents much more than its overt and urgent meaning. A picture on the other hand is subject to interpretation, the possibilities of interpretation changes with the viewpoint of the beholder. Symbols fascinate the human mind; the imagination is captured by its intrigue, and enters a process of the discovery of new meanings and insights. As you explore the various possibilities, definitions expand and concepts change. When a definition can be attached to a symbol it becomes a sign. The human mind thinks in symbols or images rather than in words.

The cross is a symbol in Christianity, when the cross is used in the form of a crucifix it becomes a sign for Catholicism. In mathematics it identifies a specific transaction, while a philosopher may consider it a crossroad. There are signs and symbols in the Bible. The Holy Spirit is identified as a dove. Understanding the meaning of a dove gives a broader perspective as to who the Holy Spirit is. For example when we think of the Holy Spirit like a dove, we picture Him as gentle, peaceful, harmless, free and alive (Matt. 3:16, 10:16). Doves are innocent and docile; they reflect the attributes of the Holy Spirit.

Another symbol of the Holy Spirit is fire. This narrates a different message; it symbolizes energy, purity, cleansing, and sanctity.

In the tabernacle the pure olive oil kept the lamp burning continually in the Holy of Holies. That was the only light behind the walled curtain and gave light for the high priest to minister to the people (Ex. 27:20-21). An offering with olive oil was a sweet savour unto the Lord. Another symbol of the Holy Spirit is oil. Oil played an important part in the lives of God's people. Olive oil was used as the holy anointing oil to consecrate the tabernacle (Ex. 40:9-16; Lev. 8) and the altar. It was used on the high priest and their sons, in food (rev. 6:6), sometimes in medicine (Mk. 6:13; James 5:14), in lamps (Matt. 25:3-8) and instruments of the sanctuary (Exodus 28:41, 30:22-33). God figuratively anointed His people (Ezekiel 16:8-9). The oil of anointing upon an individual is physical evidence that welcomes the Holy Spirit for His assigned ministry in the life of that individual.

In the induction of kings to their office (1 Sam. 10:1; 16:13; 1 Kg. 1:39; Ps. 23:5) Samuel was sent by God to anoint Israel's first king, then later David was anointed as successor even though it would be years later. We also see the change in the lives of these anointed men through the working of the Holy Spirit. The anointing opens the door for the Holy Spirit to move in His assigned work.

In the Old Testament the oil was used in the meal offering (Lev. 2:4). It is interesting to note that one offering not have olive oil poured on it was the offering relating to the trial of jealousy, "for it is an offering of jealousy, an offering of memorial, bringing iniquity to remembrance" (Numbers 5:15). And in another case, the trespass offering (Leviticus 5:11) we are told, "he shall put no oil upon it, neither shall he put any frankincense thereon: for it is a sin offering." In Psalm 23:5 the verse likens us to sheep; God the shepherd lovingly anoints their heads with oil. The use of oil during the ceremony for the cleansing of the lepers (Lev. 14:10-29), and it represents holiness, sanctification, revelation, illumination, dedication, healing, and sustaining powers. He works through material things to show Himself to the world and to bring people back to Himself.

The Holy Spirit is like oil in our lamps burning, Oil is still used in the church for anointing. At my first crusade in India, there were hundreds of bottles of oil which were up at the altar for prayer. It was my first exposure to this. However as the people increased in their faith, we witnessed the multiplication at the meetings each night as many were healed and delivered after being anointed. Families would take the oil home with them to anoint the sick and those who needed deliverance.

I was told many years ago, if I was to mail a package back to myself and it had the date registered on the postal stamps, it could be held up in court as a copyright package. This stamp proves the package has a mark or seal. Today our hands are stamped as evidence of payment to events before we can participate or have access to the benefits or privileges. Likewise the Holy Spirit is identified as a seal. His seal identifies us as a blood bought child of Christ. We enjoy the benefits and privileges bestowed upon us as children of the light. That light is a message to the world as well as the kingdom of darkness, that we have been purchased and Satan no longer has a hold on us (2 Cor. 1:22; Eph. 1:13; Eph. 4:30).

The seal indicates security, safety, ownership, authority, obligation, recognition and a finished transaction. In Acts 19:5-6 – the people of Ephesus were baptized in Christ, but Paul laid hands on them to seal them with the Holy Spirit. Rev. 9:4 tells us that the locusts could not harm those with the seal of God upon their foreheads. (Rev. 14:1 and 22:4.)

Christ identified the Holy Spirit as water. Water is a basic requirement for survival in our physical existence, so the Holy Spirit is absolutely necessary in our spiritual life. The first step of in coming to Christ is water baptism. The Word of God portrays water as a symbol, a "type" of the Spirit of God and as such is analogous to the Holy Spirit which is the divine nature of God. Jesus is also a fountain of living waters, He spoke of a spring of living water He could offer to the woman at the well, and promised her that whosoever drank of the water he offers, would never thirst again.

In John 7:36-38, Jesus proclaimed His messiahship. His warning as to where He was going and then He gave hope to those who are spiritually thirsty as He will supply divine water. After He leaves earth His work will continue through His believers, for out of their belly, rivers of living water will flow. As physical water sustains life, this living water is the source of eternal life.

At water baptism a spiritual transformation occurs signifying we are now new beings. Psalms 133:1-3 states that the Spirit is like dew. Observing plants in the evening and the morning, one will notice the revitalizing effect of the tiny mists that gently descends upon the plants and grass. The grass is fresher and of a brighter green. The dew, most time undetectable by the naked eye, gently and slowly descends during the night and is absorbed without the sometimes cruel effects of the sun, but prepares the evergreen to endure the harsh heat of the day. In the morning, depending on the humidity during the night, the mist accumulates as though it had rained.

In my encounter with the Holy Spirit, I picture Him as the dew. I see the Holy Spirit descending like dew during a service and making Himself available to those who can perceive His presence through their relationship with Him. As the dew prepares the evergreen to endure the heat of the day, so does the Holy Spirit prepare and buoys us through our unforeseen difficulties.

There are several other hallmarks of the Holy Spirit in the Bible, some more dramatic than others depending on the message to be conveyed, as events that marked the life of the prophet Elijah. Our reliance on Him is significant to His work in or through us. This demonstrates how invaluable it is not just to know the Holy Spirit but to commune with Him in all things that we do. The most innocent things can be a great work in which Jesus may be glorified. Our life should be a journey with the Holy Spirit and when we journey with Him we will find Him very good company. His outlook will afford much fruit for reflection even in silence. Our first commitment to ourselves is to pray without ceasing, meaning to continually focus on the Lord.

HARRISON S. MUNGAL

Sign as Power

Christians are encouraged to look for signs as to His Identity that He is among us (Mark 16:17). These signs shall follow them that believe. These signs include laying hands on the sick and they shall recover. Our total reliance should be on the Holy Spirit, but many start taking the credit forgetting the arm of flesh will fail. These signs of power come from the gift of the Holy Spirit endowed upon men and women of God to promote the kingdom of God and to raise Jesus higher in the hearts of men. Another evidence or sign is speaking in an unknown tongue, interpretation of tongues, or prophecy, just to list a few.

The Holy Spirit is person. (Acts 5:3,4). He is not "just the power source of God", or "just a force" nor is He "just an energy source". The Holy Spirit is God. The attributes of a person is that he has feelings, endowed with a mind, a will and speech. The Holy Spirit shares these traits but unlike a human He operates at a supernatural level. Ephesians 4:30 warns us against grieving the Holy Spirit. He grieves when His feelings are hurt. Romans 8:27 tells us that His mind is the mind of God and His knowledge is infinite, and He fulfills the will of God when He makes intercession on our behalf. In John 16:13 says, "He shall not speak of Himself, but whatsoever He shall hear, that shall He speak".

A force is abstract and do not exhibit these characteristics. A force or power cannot interact, using special abilities to satisfy different needs. When the Holy Spirit is present, we can see and feel the evidence of His power through the gifts manifested in the church. The signs are proof that the power of the Holy Spirit is real and alive. When lives are transformed from the power of darkness to the power of light there is visible evidence of the impact He makes in the life of the person He touched. His work is sometimes silent but inspiring, substantiating the work of the supernatural. Crowds answer to His silent call with no inkling what has caused them to respond as they did. Their change and passion to pursue this new calling is all the proof we need. Revivals usually produce these life transforming effects to display the power of the Almighty.

FREEDOM

WHERE THE SPIRIT is, there is freedom. No one has the monopoly on His gifts as they are free to all. This privilege does not come with established credentials. The simplest and the sophisticated can enjoy the same gifts and with the same effect as the other. God created us as free agents with a destiny designed to glorify Him. This same free will can forge the chains of bondage when we act outside the will of God. This too, is a freedom of choice. The reason for Christ to come on earth was to untangle and free us from the bondage of sin. Through the Holy Spirit we enjoy a new freedom, a freedom from guilt, shame and sin. We are now free to express ourselves in this newness of life and be partakers in God's work in the world. Satan no longer has a hold on us; God is now close and personal.

The Holy Spirit is at work when we surrender ourselves and we are aware of the mystery of allowing Him to indwell us. Our body is now His dwelling place and while He is welcome in us, He gives life and gifts. He counsels, encourages, and builds us up as we walk with Him. He steps in on our behalf and leads us to obedience. He energizes and makes effective by bringing to mind what we need to be reminded of in our walk.

We are free to express our love and our thankful-ness to God for all that He has done for us. God's plan was always for us to have a personal relationship with Him. We have the freedom to draw close, He has set no limits, and it is we who through sin distance ourselves from Him. His free gift of grace is to allow us to be close. This was His design before the foundation of the world. Our prison doors are open and the power of darkness has no hold on us. Our debt has been paid by the precious blood of Christ. Mankind was entrapped in a spiritual prison due to his sins, until

Jesus the redeemer offered Himself as the perfect sacrifice. When man confesses his sins he is pardoned.

Mercy through the free gift of grace is obtained by the merit of Christ. We as believers are free from the power of Satan's grip; however it does not mean that we are free of his temptations. The Holy Spirit will guide us in all that we do to make wise choices.

The only bondage we should have is living in a mortal body waiting to be with the Lord. When believers achieve this freedom in the Holy Spirit, we will achieve true happiness. It is living a godly life where we are given the right or the ability to live a life God designed for us. We live in bondage when we fail to follow the freedom in God. To the world, this is not freedom; freedom in Christ may appear to be more restrictive, because the world is enmity with God. The world's values differ from righteousness, man first needs to understand the reason for his birth and the consequences for his choice of action before he is able to exercise good judgment in his choice.

The seductive nature of sin appeals to the five senses, his weakness to succumb can only be overcome with the help of the Holy Spirit. This is why fellowship with Him is so vital. Without the special work of the Holy Spirit people would find excuses for their sinfulness and defend themselves against God's righteousness or the coming judgment. God use us as channels to communicate the Word of God to others, while the Holy Spirit convicts and convinces people of these truths.

A burglar does not have the freedom to steal; in the same manner a businessman does not have the freedom to avoid paying taxes. Yet both continue to struggle with the choices they have. In Christ, the only burglary that is legitimate is stealing souls from darkness into light. Lost souls are won for the kingdom of God by using the strong arm of God against the forces of evil. Satan lays claim to these souls, the man of God has to invade this territory and snatch them from the vice grips of Satan's bondage. In actual fact it is not stealing because we are all redeemed, it is Satan who continues to lie to man. He needs to be reminded of the price paid at the cross and the defeat over death through the resurrection of Christ. The scriptures attest to this truth.

Let me give you an analogy to further equate the position we are in. The freedom to breathe clean air depends on the restriction of the freedom given to factories to reduce pollution, so is it with someone depending on God with the restriction of sin even though it is within His power.

Our world revolves around corporate choices, there is no room for individuality or right over wrong. Our choices are controlled by the categories afforded to us and from which we must endorse. This type of choice is not freedom; we are coerced into thinking as a group. Distinctiveness plays no part in this corporate game of control. These limitations generate systems of bondage, tolerance level for true democracy does not exist, an Egalitarian society is impossible when man is in control. This was a privilege given to the children of Israel after they were relieved from the repressive and exploitive existence in Egypt. The freedom was not appreciated for eventually they clamored for a king like the other nations.

We find ways abscond from our responsibility so that the blame could be borne by someone else. There is no escape from our responsibility to answer to God, regardless of the circumstances around us. Choices controlled by emotions are rarely wise and very soon the after effects of the consequences leave a trail of bitterness and resentment. When our choice is based on sound doctrine there is never a need to justify the outcome because we know who is in control.

When I think of a Libertarian, I see one who would define freedom for the 'might' of the country. A Socialist on the other hand defines freedom in terms of being free from hunger, sickness and shelter. The Church views freedom as having everything and free to choose what is needed for life. Freedom gives a person ownership to choose. A slave who has acquired freedom can choose where he wants to go and who he wants to work for. He will remember the oppression and rigid demands impinged on him and ideally he should appreciate and cherish his freedom more than someone who was never had to succumb and be obedient to this tyrannical rule. Yet by virtue of having been in bondage the choices before him is never viewed in the same light as one born free.

The Bible makes it clear that we were all like slaves, until Jesus paid the price for our freedom. We know we are free but do not act as free men. Our thinking has to be converted and this is a process. There are different stages in our conversion before we fully grasp the freedom in Christ. We are not rid of the shame and guilt immediately, yet we do know where to go when these feelings haunts us. The Holy Spirit will comfort us as we grow in the Lord. Like a soldier who knows his country is backing him one hundred percent, so is the child in Christ. This gives freedom to live!

There is a freedom in equality. In the world system, in the workforce the employer has power over an employee; In governments the president or ruler wields his power over the country, in commerce the vender has power through his product and in society the law has power over its citizen, while the owner of an estate exercise his rights to occupy it as he pleases. The kingdom of God is classless, uncensored and free. Everyone is equal in God's eyes. He does not judge by your ethnicity, your economic status, or by your gender. Everyone has access to the same blessings and privileges.

From the world's point of view freedom comes by a debt we owe. In God's kingdom freedom comes without a cost, for the price has been paid. Living in freedom does not mean a carefree life with no obstacles. We will be faced with trials and dangers and we are required to be accountable and to accept responsibility for the choices we make. Our choice to serve God rather than the world comes at a cost that many are not prepared to pay, but in comparing the benefits from serving the King of Kings many would die for the privilege.

Freedom can only be offered by a higher authority. For example if it pertains to the land, the government is in control to enforce the law. If it pertains to employment, the employer exercises this right. If it pertains to us in Christ, it can only come from God Himself.

HARRISON S. MUNGAL

It was the fall of 2005 when I grasped the full picture of what freedom looked like in the world. One of my daughters fainted in school and was taken to the hospital. My wife arrived at 14:20hrs at the hospital and I came around 40 minutes later to relieve my wife so that she could be at home with the rest of our children. While waiting, our daughter appeared to be OK. I approached one of the nurses and asked her if it was possible for my daughter to be released and I will take her to our family doctor the following day. She agreed with me that all my daughter's vital signs were OK, and that her fainting could have been caused by lack of eating breakfast. She advised me that I should consult the triage nurse and let her know of our discussion.

I did as instructed, however the nurse at the desk was not cooperative. In fact she was adamant that I remain at the hospital, she retorted "otherwise I will call in Children's Aid". I did not retaliate; instead I called my wife and informed her of the current position. My nine year old daughter and I waited over six hours; at 23:00 hrs I realized that we were the last ones in the waiting room among those who had come in around the same time I did. I enquired at the front desk as to the reason my daughter was not getting any medical attention. Her reply was, "her file is not here?" We waited while she searched; finally she came back reporting that she found a copy of our file in the trash and a note stating that we had left the hospital and that CAS was contacted. I became livid; I then requested a copy of their video tape as this was falsified documentation. Immediately, she ordered a CAT scan for my daughter. When we got there the technician advised that he could not administer the CAT scan because it was not approved by a medical doctor. He called front desk and was given the go ahead. Eventually she was seen and assessed by the ER doctor at 1:15 hrs. His diagnosis was exactly the same as originally given over eight hours earlier. He then apologized for the misunderstanding and advised me to contact the staff supervisor.

For the first time I realized with all the knowledge, experience and authority I had as a clinician and citizen, I was helpless, I was a victim of internal bureaucracy of medi-care system that left me powerless over my own child. The following morning a CAS worker called requesting information about all our children including my wife and me. After explaining the situation, she suggested that we contact the hospital ombudsman as well as the medical director. The frustration and loss of time not to mention the embarrassment we went through were the direct result of one nurse who felt she had power over me and wanted to enforce it. The hospital had a video tape confirming that my daughter and I were at the waiting room for over 8 hours. There was no verbal or written apologies made and my daughter and I were powerless to exercise our rights as victims of circumstance. We were stripped of our freedom and dignity as citizens of our so called free society.

With God, this is totally different. God holds all power and authority and He gives freedom to all who accept the fact that Jesus Christ died for the sins of the world. The Holy Spirit enforces this authority to the Church, and only when we realize that we have this freedom we can operate in it. This freedom is gained through knowledge, experience and understanding God's principles. The greatest freedom anyone can have is being free from sin.

When one understands the freedom acquired from salvation in Christ, appreciation results in a deep desire to be close to God and a relationship with the Holy Spirit develops. It is futile living a life without God. Everything in life loses its value, when we realize the reason we live is not for self but to love and serve the Great I Am, and the knowledge that we will be with Him forever. Forever is a long time, so we better become use to it. Knowing Him now is the key to be prepared for eternity.

FOREVER WITH HIM

1 Cor. 3:16-17

THE HOLY SPIRIT abides in us. There are numerous spirits, but there is only one Holy Spirit. Our body the temple could not become holy just by attending church every Sunday, or by subscribing to a good cause or by writing a cheque. We can only become holy through the blood of Jesus Christ which means we have to first believe in Jesus as our Lord and saviour and only then we have the protection of His precious blood. In order to stay holy, there must be a relationship with the one who lives and dwells within, we continue in our holiness as this relationship becomes more meaningful and intimate with God's Holy Spirit. There are no short cuts, no comprising. He wants all of you.

God has made it possible for His Spirit to dwell in us. The requirement is staying in fellowship with Him. We are so caught up in the mundane things of life that we forget to spend time with the most important person in our life and that is the Holy Spirit. We often depend on others to do the praying for us instead of going to God first. The scriptures contain prophetic words to build our faith and help us to trust in Him who gave us these promises and believe that He will deliver that which He has promised. Our dependence on the physical should never take precedence over the spiritual. Flesh will fail but the Spirit never does, not if it is the Spirit of God. God wants all His children to have a personal relationship with Him and this image is reflected in our earthly parents who desire for their children to come to them first rather than their friends.

We tend to forget that we have free access to our Heavenly Father at all times. Instead the first option we exercise is worry, then to go to our doctor, pay exorbitant fees for advice and on prescriptions and only when all else fails and we are left in a financial deficit position do we come to God. His service is free. He gladly mends our broken state though His healing and miracles. Through His salvation we are rescued from our miserable state. We are comforted with the peace of mind that transcends human understanding. The only requirement is faith and trust in our Saviour and to understand His grace is sufficient for us. The Holy Spirit longs for us to trust Him but instead we reject His help until we are cornered and all worldly avenues have failed. He longs for us to witness His supernatural power. As much as it takes time to discover the power of love, it takes time to know the Holy Spirit.

I remember after getting married, there were so many little things I still did not know about my wife Kathleen and it was the same with her towards me. However as I spent quality time with her, we became more transparent to each other. As we grew together our love and trust deepened, this became a powerful tool in the relationship to take us through rough patches.

The key to God's heart is to love Him with every fibre of our being. Love can only develop when there is a relationship of trust. We cannot make love happen, it is a process and involves work. No pretentious emotion will endure. This love is tested and only genuine love will stand up to the persistent attacks that assail us. Flesh alone cannot withstand the assaults; it is only when we surrender our will to God that the Holy Spirit can function on our behalf.

We do not have to look far to realize how easy it is for us to succumb to temptation. It takes every fibre of our being to resist the enticement to go contrary to the will of God. Being a Christian does not immune us from temptation, the battle is even greater for those who profess Christ as their Lord and Saviour. Satan does not want Him to be glorified; Jesus is lover of our souls while Satan is the destroyer. The Holy Spirit will bring to remembrance the Word of God which is the sword of the Spirit as our defence against the wiles of the devil. This is why it is important to study the Word of God so we can use it as a guard and protection. The word vindicates us against Satan's accusations.

It is unusual for someone to surrender something of value to someone without expecting something in return. There are numerous reports of things being taken without permission. Cars are stolen, fraudulent withdrawals from bank account, and forced entry into homes depriving individuals of valuable assets and life savings. We accept theft as a fact of life and use all types of security systems to protect our material assets but when someone surrenders something of value to another especially Christians, the criticisms of the ulterior motive of the Christian is under scrutiny. Yet many Christians have given up financial opportunities in order to be in service of the Lord. The giver also is subjected to suspicion of the soundness of their minds to perform this unnatural act of giving generously. The worlds system is in direct opposition to the spiritual way of life; however, we expect great things from God and His ministers without giving anything of ourselves.

When I think of the power of the Holy Spirit, this analogy comes to mind. I think of the Spirit as living water, Christians as the water hose and Christ as the source of the water. For us to receive the water the hose has to be connected to the source before we can have access to the water. Then we receive the benefits the water provides like keeping us clean or quenching our thirst. The closer our relationship is with God, the stronger the pressure is in releasing the flow of water to us. Unfortunately, there are many obstacles that can get in our way, creating blockages to stop the flow. If we are not connected properly to the main source, it makes it impossible for the flow of the Holy Spirit and this happens when there is sin in our lives. Then we learn that a steady pressure is needed to keep the nozzle open. The hose is put in by faith knowing there is water but faith without works is dead. When we have the faith that there is water then we have to step out to receive the water or the water remains in the hose.

This is when the miracle happens; when the water comes forth it is applied for different purposes. The water is then applied to various uses that can be seen as the gifts of the Spirit. It can be used for household purposes, preparing meals, cleaning, watering a garden, supply food to the recipients, help others as well as to fill reservoirs for others to use through the miracle of faith. The man or woman of God has the anointing to apply to the sick or to perform miracles. It is amazing to see how far this water can reach. The greater the pressure, the greater the power, the further the water can reach and touch. The cleaner our lives become, the greater the pressure and the power it holds. When we are filled with the Holy Spirit, the work of God is manifested through the lives of righteous men and women winning souls and brings Glory to God.

Water is a source of life, without it there is no growth, death and disease is inevitable. Similarly, without the Holy Spirit man will not be able to fight against the adversary. Our flesh is no match for Satan; without the Holy Spirit we will be in spiritual darkness and death and destruction will be our ultimate end. Jesus promised never to leave us comfortless, He promised us the Holy Spirit as the comforter through whom we will receive living waters. The rest is up to us to willingly surrender our will to God to do as He sees fit. Just the knowledge of the source and what it can do for us is not enough. We have to let go and surrender ourselves in His capable hands.

There is a vast difference between having water flow through us and water falling on us. When I think of the great Niagara Falls I realize that for centuries the water has been falling over the cliff. As the water flows over the cliff onto the great rocks below it has no impact on the inside of this huge rock. If it were possible to stop the flow of the water and crack the gigantic rock open it would look no different inside then a rock that had been out in the sun for centuries. Looking inside this gigantic rock which had been sitting under the great falls for hundreds of years you notice that it is completely dry inside. Not a drop of water penetrated its surface. Like the water of Niagara Falls, the Holy Spirit moves upon and touches our life, but never flows through us. I believe it is time to have an encounter with the Holy Spirit. He is looking for ordinary vessels like you and I. Imperfect vessels, hurt vessels, raw material, waiting to avail themselves.

HARRISON S. MUNGAL

Forever With Him

When we consent to the Holy Spirit to be in partnership with us, the development is purely beautiful. Working with the Holy Spirit is similar to how the rose progresses from bud to a full fledged flower. Like the gifts of the Holy Spirit each petal unfurls in slow progress veiled from the naked eye, yet progressively shapes its destiny. Each stage signals greater expectations until as a full blown flower man and the birds, bees and the insects come to enjoy its sweet nectar as the aromatic perfume fills the air beckoning us with the promise we long for. The grandeur of this magnificent beauty does not stay with us for long. If we fail to appreciate this mystical bloom because we are taken up with seemingly important matters of the world, we find in our return only the trace of what was as evidenced by scattered petals and a withered calyx on the stem. The sweet perfume that once invaded the atmosphere has now evaporated with no trace of its ambience. If time will be kind to us we may catch a glimpse of another bloom.

Our walk with the Lord and our born again experience is parallel to the development of the rose from bud to maturity. It is an unforgettable experience and our coach the Holy Spirit is instrumental in setting the mood of the occurrence that will shape our lives forever. A true born again event is never forgotten; it transforms lives in a visible way that others may recognise. The different degree to which we develop from this day is defined by our involvement in heeding the lesson given by our coach. The Holy Spirit will be with us until the end of our earthly life.

For many of us activity suggests a purposeful life. Aging is a natural process and as hard as man may try to reverse the process it is a fight against nature. Aging brings us face to face with our mortality, this is a fact and it cannot be denied. Likewise we should gracefully surrender the things of our youth. As we age we are more susceptible to the voice of the Holy Spirit. Proverbs 22:6 admonishes parents "Train up a child in the way he should go: and when he is old, he will not depart from it". (KJV)

Whatever the physical appearance of the outward man, the internal workings continue to be affected by age regardless. Our dim sight, dull hearing, slow reflexes, declining memory and the wear and tear of our internal organs are evidence of age. Our every effort to keep young will not hold us on earth one day longer than our appointed time. Understanding that life on earth is temporal, leading to a transition into a spiritual being. It is important we realize that while on earth we are to prepare for the life to come. From the time we are accountable for our sins our conscience guides us to fulfil the purpose for which we were created. God created this built in mechanism as a tool for our defence against sin. This eventually brings us to the consciousness of the work of the Spirit, until the choice to invite Him in our lives is exercised. He never comes uninvited but once we open the doors to Him He coaches us in all things including the joy we will have in being with the Lord, living forever in eternity with Him.

SAVOUR THE FRAGRANCE

MOST OF US are familiar with the story of the Alabaster Box (Matthew 26:6-13; John 12:1-8; Mark 14:3-9). This story holds some power lessons. One day I was reading this story when I gleaned some light into the power of the fragrance. We know there are various scents and each can be identified as to its origin. For example some people use specific perfumes and those familiar with their preference of cologne can tell of their presence even though their physical presence is not yet identified. I can tell my wife's fragrance anywhere it seems, her perfume together with her body chemistry produce an aroma uniquely hers. Similarly flowers exude an odour into the atmosphere and without seeing the source we know that a specific flowering shrub is in the vicinity.

Similarly the Holy Spirit lets His presence be known by a sweet aromatic scent that identifies Him. Through the Spirit of discernment we can recognize the presence of the Holy Spirit in our midst. In like manner we recognize the evil odour of the enemy. We are prepared accordingly to either welcome and entertain when it is the Holy Spirit or be prepared for spiritual warfare when it is the enemy.

This brings to mind the alabaster box incident. Both Matthew and Mark record the incident as the spikenard ointment being poured on Jesus' head while John's record mentions the ointment being used to anoint His feet. Our Lord's reply was that the pouring of this ointment on His body was symbolic of His burial. It seems to transfer the spiritual responsibility from Jesus to the Holy Spirit starting from His burial and the part the Holy Spirit played in His resurrection.

As oil in the lamp that gives light to our path is symbolic of the presence of the Holy Spirit and the revelation He brings to believers, the scent of the spikenard we are told filled the house with the odour of the ointment. This tells of the potency of the aroma, like the Holy Spirit once released can not be contained but His fragrance like a burst of energy will fill the atmosphere. Jesus was confined to a specific location by His physical body. He could not be omnipresent but through the Holy Spirit He could be known to as many that call on Him at the same time. Through ones discernment He could be recognized as oil in the anointing, the movement of the wind, the symbol of water, the sweet aroma, a light or the symbol of the dove.

The costly spikenard is representative of the price to be paid by our Lord before mankind can enjoy the luxury of this priceless gift to humanity. The washing of His feet by the tears of this sinner indicates our state of brokenness before the Lord in public confession and the humility required. The hair with which she wiped His feet signifies the letting down of pride in the presence of the Holy Spirit before He fills our being. Those present in the house of Simon the leper were not there because they came to hear Jesus, but to see Lazarus who was raised from the dead. They focused their attention on the sins of Mary who lavished her love on our Lord rather than higher spiritual aspects of the act she performed.

In this episode it is revealed that those who condemned her act of benevolence were too involved with material things. They lacked the understanding of man's sinful nature by comparing themselves with this woman's worthiness being deemed a sinner. Our Lord's rebuke to Simon, who did not do the basic hospitable thing of the day by washing his guest's feet, portrays the false pride and their sense of superiority. The action of this woman exposed their false sense of security attained by observing the law. They failed to recognize and appreciate the quality fellowship of our Lord whose physical presence would soon be taken away from them.

We can feel the supernatural power of Holy Spirit around us, with a sense of authority as passed from our Lord to Him as He promised. Like those in the house of Simon the leper in Bethany, many Christians miss the moment the Holy Spirit attend us; by our thoughts on worldly matters which form obstacles in distinguishing the change in our environment. If we become more familiar and sensitive to His presence, we will relish the moment and rise to the occasion in which His power can be manifested in bringing others to saving faith and giving God the Glory by the signs and wonders that follow. This becomes more evident when our prayer life is more meaningful and our relationship grows closer; then our sensitivity to His presence is more acute. This does not happen overnight but is a process that prepares us as our senses to higher spiritual things are sharpened.

A prayerful life will help us detect the work of the enemy who tries to obstruct and impede our involvement with the Holy Spirit. The Holy Spirit Himself will help us avoid these hindrances when we are in tune with Him. He will provide us with the spiritual ammunition needed to keep us in line with Him. We cannot afford to take things for granted since Satan is a master and he employs any means to accomplish his mission.

Our past experiences when we were outwitted by Satan in thinking we can are equipped to deal with him, are lessons for us to admit our weaknesses and to rely on the Holy Spirit. In every encounter that He presents to us we grow stronger and wiser. When we are defeated it is not a lesson lost but preparation to meet Him at another level when we eventually resign ourselves to our Coach and counsellor. Being in the Word is our ammunition against the enemy. The Word is the sword of the spirit and the Holy Spirit will bring it to remembrance when we are in need of it against any attack. It is expected for us to draw on His power and this in turn is a tool in drawing lost souls to Christ.

PREPARATION

PREPARATION IS ATTENTION and time spent in accessing all situations at hand. Then prioritizing situations by importance in one's life, and then setting goals as to how these goals will be materialized. This is not as simple as it sounds. Commitment is an indication of the seriousness of the task ahead; a strategy is set with the appropriate time necessary and a dedication to start immediately. Tomorrow is never a good time to start since tomorrow is still always a day away. If now is inappropriate then a date on the calendar will do, remembering there is no guarantee life will permit us to see that day. Here again life does not allow us to work on one situation at a time, there are other needs that run concurrently with the goals set, e.g. at the desk working one still has to eat and do other things that nature demands, then there is time out to stretch and relax in order that we may be productive at the task. Similarly spiritual needs cannot be isolated from our physical needs and commitment to family and society.

To succeed in accomplishing one's goal by priority, attention has to be paid to the individual as a whole and a balance should be set where one area does not suffer at the expense of another. I remember when I made a resolution to dedicate one year for the Lord in constant prayer. I had to discipline myself, to counteract my weakness of early morning prayer.

Preparation for me involved placing a loud alarm clock in another room. This way I was not tempted to turn it off like when it was on the night table. When it went off I had to scurry over to the other room to turn it off so that it would not disturb the rest of the family. I had my worship music close to the alarm clock which I would set to play. This activity tended to take me out of my sleepy mode, by the time I freshened up I was wide awake and enter into prayer and worship. The time spent with the Holy Spirit in prayer proved quite fruitful. This took away the stress of trying too hard to make myself pray. I was relaxed and gently allowed myself to obediently follow the will of the spirit.

When one makes a vow to pray for an hour or so every day, they should not feel the pressure of being bound. Just relaxing in His presence and answering the gentle voice within will be more beneficial, otherwise it will not last and we end up dissatisfied with our prayer life. Others may face the same problem as I did and when the alarm goes off they turn over, turn it off and go back to sleep. God's plan is for us to come willingly to Him and enjoy being in His presence. At the same time we have to discipline ourselves in areas unfamiliar to us. We need to learn how to crawl before we can walk; this is similar to lifting weights. We start with what we are comfortable with then stretch ourselves gradually towards our goal.

I encourage people to maintain a prayer life starting with 15 minutes a day for a week or two. Being consistent is important; as time goes by you will enjoy His presence and gradually you will increase in your time spent with God. Some may have to consciously increase their time spent in prayer. The key is surrendering yourself to the Holy Spirit and before you know it time no longer matters you're your relationship with Him is developed you will hunger to be with Him. It's like courting, absence from each other lets the heart grow fonder and the reunion is always wonderful. It may seem like a lot of work, but commitment and responsible bears fruits of power with maturity.

God's glory comes from much personal sacrifice, the condition of the heart and purity of mind are the determining factors and these qualities are not easily attained. A dire thirst and passion will help us to perseverance in prayer, fasting, studying His Word, and labouring in building our character in the fruit of the spirit. These are the hallmarks of individuals through whom God's Glory are usually manifested. We must be worthy vessels through which God will demonstrate Himself. Jesus Christ has left the footprints of the path we are to take in this pilgrimage and only a love for Him will take us there.

We must dedicate time to be in His presence. As we sing and dance before Him the time spent in praise and worship allows us to commune with the Holy Spirit and He takes us to the throne room of the King of Kings and the Lord of Lords. Here we appreciate His holiness, His power and His might. It brings us to the consciousness of our weak frame and to realize the work done for us by our Saviour. The thanksgiving for this gift to mankind is reciprocated by offering Him our heart of love.

Jesus left a blueprint for us to follow in the form of the Lord's Prayer. We first address Him as 'Our Father', meaning we are all brothers and God is the Father of us all. He then brings us to the awareness of who He is, He is Holy so is His name, because of this we approach Him with reverence and respect. He is all mighty and we are but dust and ashes in His sight. It is He who considers us worthy of Him and allows us to be partakers in His kingdom and this only occurs when we surrender ourselves to His will. It is only after these preliminaries that we should consider our personal needs. Many of us come to Him asking favours without the kind courtesy of acknowledging Him for who He is. This is a sign of a lack of humility.

The only reason we can stand in His presence is because we are covered in the blood of Jesus. We are unworthy of His favour and it is only though His grace that we are saved. These are potent reasons to compel us to be thankful for being recipients of His grace. We need to show our appreciation to His Son through whom we are now adopted sons and have the privilege of calling Him Abba, a most endearing term for Father. The qualities acquired through Jesus are that we are no longer in bondage but are free. Through Him we are more than a conqueror. He chose us before the foundation of this world, and loved us while we were yet in sin. He promised us that no weapon formed against us shall prosper.

Meditating on these qualities will bring us into His presence. We react when He is present in different ways; none of which we have any control. The Holy Spirit intercedes on our behalf. We also should not come with our agenda or expectation as to how He will respond, in fact weeks may go by before we start feeling His presence in a real way. As mentioned earlier sincerity and purity of heart will bring us closer to God. There must be a Father/child relationship before He responds and relationship takes time to build; lip service will accomplish nothing. The quality of time spend in His presence will move Him. The sooner we can bare our heart and soul before Him the more effective our prayer becomes.

ANOINTING

"But the anointing which ye have received of him abideth in you, and ye need not that any man teach you: but as the same anointing teacheth you of all things,"
1 John 2:27

THIS WORD *"ANOINTING"* has brought about all kinds of ideas in the church and the various denominations. Some consider it mysterious and others have a vague idea of the concept. I was very young when I ventured out into the ministry and almost every service I ministered in, the leaders would do two things. They would ask how old I was, and then they would pray for the "anointing" to be poured out upon me as I minister the Word of the Lord. I feel that when someone is called, the anointing of that gift is upon him. It is the minister's life with God that allows the flow of the anointing. This does not mean the man of God should not be prayed for but it is not something that can be willed on him. God is the giver of all gifts according to His riches in glory.

When the atmosphere is right and all are in one accord, the glory of God will manifest itself by ushering the presence of God to reach our world. Most churches speak about it; teach us about the power it holds and how it came about in the Old Testament. We hear that "the anointing breaks the yokes of bondage", what does this mean? And how do we acquire this power?

"the yoke shall be destroyed because of the anointing". Isaiah 10:27

The analogy of the yoke is a wooden implement placed around an animal's neck, to physically control the animal. This allows the owner to manipulate and direct the animal to do his bidding. The above verse refers to our spiritual yoke that restricts our movement with God's. It is the anointing that breaks the yoke and brings freedom to move in the Spirit. From a Biblical perspective, we have learnt that Kings and priests were ceremonially anointed and set apart, usually by prophets. Oil was used as a seal by making a mark or being poured upon the individual as a physical sign of the anointing. The person has to be recognized for being in the state of faithful obedience to his calling and position. The practice of specially prepared ointment was common among the Hebrews.

The significance of anointing was symbolic of consecration for a holy or sacred use; hence the anointing of the high priest (Ex 29:29; Lev 4:3) and of the sacred vessels (Ex 30:26). The high priest and the king are thus called "the anointed" (Lev 4:3, Lev 4:5, Lev 4:16; Lev 6:20; Ps 132:10). Anointing a king was equivalent to crowning him (1Sam16:13; 2Sam 2:4, etc.). Prophets were also anointed (1Kings 19:16; 1Chr 16:22; Ps 105:15).

The expression, "anoint the shield" (Isa 21:5), refers to the custom of rubbing oil on the leather of the shield so as to make it supple and fit for use in war. Anointing was also an act of hospitality (Luke 7:38, Luke 7:46). It was the custom of the Jews in like manner to anoint themselves with oil, as a means of refreshing or invigorating their bodies (Deut 28:40; Ruth 3:3; 2Sam 14:2; Ps 104:15, etc.). This custom is continued among the Arabs to this present day. Oil was also used for medicinal purposes. It was applied to the sick, and also to wounds (Isa 1:6; Mark 6:13; James 5:14).

The bodies of the dead were sometimes anointed (Mark 14:8; Luke 23:56). The promised delivered is twice called the "Anointed" or Messiah (Ps 2:2; Dan 9:25, Dan 9:26), because he was anointed with the Holy Ghost (Isa 61:1), figuratively styled the "oil of gladness" (Ps 45:7; Heb 1:9). Jesus of Nazareth is this anointed One (John1:41; Acts9:22; Acts17:2, Acts17:3; Acts18:5, Acts18:28), the Messiah of the Old Testament.

In the New Testament, the anointing comes in richness when the Holy Spirit is present. Our fellowship and relationship with the Holy Spirit opens the doorway for the power of the anointing to be released.

> *"The Spirit of the Lord is upon me, because he hath anointed me to preach the gospel to the poor; he hath sent me to heal the brokenhearted, to preach deliverance to the captives, and recovering of sight to the blind, to set at liberty them that are bruised,"* Luke 4:18.

There is a purpose for the anointing of God. We are anointed to preach the gospel, heal the broken hearted, preach deliverance, open blind eyes and bring freedom. Anointing is not to be toyed with, or use for vain glory towards our own personal gain. It is to be used to build the kingdom of God.

The anointing is given to preach the gospel to the poor, to bring the revelation of God's love to those who are seeking. God's anointing flows to those who are hungry for a touch from His Holy Spirit. The anointing has less to do with the person that it flows through than it does with the person who receives it, and the One who sent it, God Almighty. (Luke 6:19-20 NKJV) the whole multitude sought to touch Him, for power went out from Him and healed them all. Then He lifted up His eyes toward His disciples, and said: *"Blessed are the poor, for yours is the kingdom of God."*

"Blessed are the poor in spirit, for theirs is the kingdom of heaven". Matthew 5:3 NKJV. The term poor here is the Greek word, ptochos which carries the implication of being a beggar, in this case a spiritual beggar hungry for the Spirit of God.

The anointing can be stifled if the people refuse to receive it from the person that God is sending it through. Things such as pride, envy, bitterness, and unforgiveness against an anointed person can prevent the receiver from accepting it. The anointed person must be directed to people that can receive it.

> *"So they were offended at Him. But Jesus said to them, A prophet is not without honor except in his own country and in his own house. Now He did not do many mighty works in His home town because of their unbelief."* Matthew 13:57-58 NKJV

> *"If the household is worthy, let your peace come upon it. But if it is not worthy, let your peace return to you. And whoever will not receive you nor hear your words, when you depart from that house or city, shake off the dust from your feet".* Matthew 10:13-14 NKJV

The anointing is given to heal and restore people. We see this happening throughout the Bible, particularly in the life of Christ and the early apostles. *"The word which God sent to the children of Israel, preaching peace through Jesus Christ; He is Lord of all; that word you know, which was proclaimed throughout all Judea, and began from Galilee after the baptism which John preached: how God anointed Jesus of Nazareth with the Holy Spirit and with power, who went about doing good and healing all who were oppressed by the devil, for God was with Him".* Acts 10:36-38 NKJV

The anointing is given to proclaim freedom to the captives. When one is anointed there is no fear of the unknown. They acquire an internal freedom to step beyond their boundaries. They have a way of speaking to people with the authority of the Lord as the Word permeates them. (2 Timothy 2:24-26 NKJV) And a servant of the Lord must not quarrel but be gentle to all, able to teach, patient, in humility correcting those who are in opposition, if God perhaps will grant them repentance, so that they may know the truth, and that they may come to their senses and escape the snare of the devil, having been taken captive by him to do his will.

The anointing is given to open blind eyes. When one is anointed, the Word of God that flows from their lips touches minds; this in turn affects those who are spiritually blind. I have seen it done many times in my crusades. The anointing will reveal truth; the Rhema of God will be received. I believe the reason Jesus was able to touch so many lives on earth, was the mere fact that He was able to open their eyes to truth when He preached the Word. *"But even if our gospel is veiled, it is veiled to those who are perishing, whose minds the god of this age has blinded, who do not believe, lest the light of the gospel of the glory of Christ, who is the image of God, should shine on them.* "2 Corinthians 4:3-4 NKJV

> *"I counsel you to buy from Me gold refined in the fire, that you may be rich; and white garments, that you may be clothed, that the shame of your nakedness may not be revealed; and anoint your eyes with eye salve, that you may see".* Revelation 3:18 NKJV

The anointing is given to set people free. God has entrusted us with His anointing to set souls free from the power of darkness. People are blinded by the god of this world, and the anointing is the antidote for sin. It has always been the remedy to set people free from bondages. *"It shall come to pass in that day that his burden will be taken away from your shoulder, And his yoke from your neck, And the yoke will be destroyed because of the anointing oil."* Isaiah 10:27 NKJV

> *"Therefore if the Son makes you free, you shall be free indeed".* John 8:36 NKJV

> *"For we are His workmanship, created in Christ Jesus for good works, which God prepared beforehand that we should walk in them. As we walk in the anointing of God we go where God wills, do what God wills, and say what God wills."* Ephesians 2:10 NKJV

Then Jesus said to them, *"When you lift up the Son of Man, then you will know that I am He, and that I do nothing of Myself; but as My Father taught Me, I speak these things. And He who sent Me is with Me. The Father has not left Me alone, for I always do those things that please Him."* John 8:28-29 NKJV

The anointing of the Holy Spirit is a gift from God. This gift is given when He can trust us with it. It is one of His most precious gifts. Jesus answered and said to the woman at the well, *"If you knew the gift of God, and who it is who says to you, 'Give Me a drink,' you would have asked Him, and He would have given you living water."* John 4:10 NKJV

Jesus answered and said to her, *"Whoever drinks of this water will thirst again, but whoever drinks of the water that I shall give him will never thirst. But the water that I shall give him will become in him a fountain of water springing up into everlasting life."* John 4:13-14 NKJV

On the last day, that great day of the feast, Jesus stood and cried out, saying, *"If anyone thirsts, let him come to Me and drink. He who believes in Me, as the Scripture has said, out of his heart will flow rivers of living water. But this He spoke concerning the Spirit, whom those believing in Him would receive; for the Holy Spirit was not yet given, because Jesus was not yet glorified."* John 7:37-39 NKJV

> "For all the promises of God in Him are Yes, and in Him Amen, to the glory of God through us. Now He who establishes us with you in Christ and has anointed us is God, who also has sealed us and given us the Spirit in our hearts as a guarantee."
> 2 Corinthians 1:20-22 NKJV

The anointing gives wisdom. Through the anointing we exercise wisdom. It will help us to demonstrate the call upon our lives. It will teach us how to handle difficult situations which in the natural may seem impossible. *"But you have an anointing from the Holy One, and you know all things."* 1 John 2:20 NKJV

> "*But the anointing which you have received from Him abides in you, and you do not need that anyone teach you; but as the same anointing teaches you concerning all things, and is true, and is not a lie, and just as it has taught you, you will abide in Him.*" 1 John 2:27 NKJV

> "*The Spirit of the LORD shall rest upon Him, The Spirit of wisdom and understanding, The Spirit of counsel and might, The Spirit of knowledge and of the fear of the LORD.*" Isaiah 11:2 NKJV

> "*Those who are wise shall shine Like the brightness of the firmament, And those who turn many to righteousness Like the stars forever and ever.*" Daniel 12:3 NKJV

> "*The fruit of the righteous is a tree of life, And he who wins souls is wise.*" Proverbs 11:30 NKJV

> "*So teach us to number our days, That we may gain a heart of wisdom.*" Psalms 90:12 NKJV

> "*How precious is Your loving kindness, O God! Therefore the children of men put their trust under the shadow of Your wings. They are abundantly satisfied with the fullness of Your house, And You give them drink from the river of Your pleasures. For with You is the fountain of life; In Your light we see light.*" Psalms 36:7-9 NKJV

> "*the anointing you have received from Him abides in you . . . . the same anointing teaches you concerning all things . . . .*". 1 John 2:27

Whoever is born again and has a relationship with the Holy Spirit has a measure of anointing upon them. The anointing will open the doors of opportunity. It comes from a hunger in the hearts of those who seek God. Without the anointing, battles are not won, and our walk in Christ becomes a tedious one. The anointing will release the Rhema Word; it will create a conviction in our heart to follow truth. We will live by the gifts of the Spirit walking daily in His fruits.

"Touch Not My anointed ones, and do My prophets no harm." Ps 105:15

When God told Saul (His anointed) to *"Smite Amalek, and utterly destroy all that they have, and spare them not . . ."* (1 Sam. 15:3) Saul disobeyed and *"spared the best of the sheep and of the oxen, to sacrifice unto the Lord . . ."* (v.15). Samuel wasted no time in publicly denouncing Saul's for his disobedience, rebuking him because *"rebellion is as the sin of witchcraft".* (v.23), and that God had rejected him as king. The Lord's 'anointed' was verbally condemned by Samuel for his disobedience.

The anointing on someone's life is a very serious matter. When God sanctions an anointing it is only for Him to negate that endorsement. No matter how badly the anointed person has deviated from the ways of God or however great the digression in our eyes or the effect of his conduct on the lives of others, it is not in our power to hurt or decry or defame that person. We need to seek God's wisdom in handling the situation around us. The person of authority is still to be respected until God removes him. God is always in control. The story of David and Saul is a compelling story of the Lord's anointed who has blatantly transgressed God's laws and abused his privileges as king.

We, as mortal beings, should learn from the life of David whose life was threatened and who had to live a life of exile because of one man's sheer jealousy. He had many opportunities to harm King Saul but resisted even though he was being pursued as a fugitive. David was not even tempted when the opportunity presented itself; in fact he was full of remorse for cutting the king's skirt while he lay fast asleep and at the mercy of his opponent. The indelible words of David to his pursuer should be etched in our hearts when we are faced with circumstances in life. Our own self pity can be our undoing. Let the words of David resound in our situation and let us pray his words *"Who can stretch out his hand against the Lord's anointed, and be guiltless?"* (I Sam 26: 3-11).

In verse 15-16 David even rebuked Abner for not guarding Saul and says he deserved to die for not protecting his master. However it did not prohibit David from reminding Saul that he was unjust in hounding him since he was innocent and had done nothing to harm Saul. Saul by his own admission in repenting of his action, called himself a fool. Saul declared that he would not harm David any more since he realized how dear his life was in David's eyes. In returning Saul's possessions David remarked, *"For the Lord delivered you into my hand but I would not stretch out my hand against the Lord's anointed."* (vs 17-24).

The story of Saul ends in a battle in which David had no part and in which both Saul and Jonathan lost their lives. The news of this tragedy was not music to David's ears. The heroic act of the Amalakite messenger that he killed Saul was not received as glad tidings, instead he was sharply rebuked by David *"How was it you were not afraid to put forth your hand to destroy the Lord's anointed?"* then David summoned one of his men and said, *"Go near, and execute him!"* The so called valiant act of this Amalakite cost him his life. And David pronounced that *"Your blood is on your own head, for your own mouth has testified against you, saying, 'I have killed the Lord's anointed.'"* (2 Sam 1:13-16).

We should respect the anointing and never abuse it. Respect those who have it flowing though them and explore the opportunity to absorb as much as possible. The Holy Spirit will coach you into all the possible ways in gaining access to this anointing in order for the ministry to flourish.

OUR POSITION

"To Him who loved us and washed us from our sins in His own blood, and has made us kings and priests to His God and Father, to Him be glory and dominion forever and ever. Amen." (Revelation 1:5, 6)

OUR ULTIMATE POSITION in the kingdom of God is to assume the role of a king and priest. Only through the power of God is it possible and through the Holy Spirit is it possible to take the positions we are called to. We were sanctified by the precious blood of Christ and anointed by the Holy Spirit to take the offices as kings and priests. The believer is now equipped with power to exercise the authority given him in administering the responsibilities of his assigned office he has now been ordained to function in. His work can only be effective when he operates in the authority and power of the Holy Spirit.

All too often the church has compromised or diluted these dominant truths. Emerging theologies have been crafted with cunning deceptions which grossly misconstrue what God has ordained for man. The introduction of a Holy order was a devise to separate the clergy from the congregation. Some theories indicate that one could be a king or a priest, but not both. Others talk of a common priesthood to theologians but it means very little in their lives, and yet others support that the idea of the believer having any kind of kingly power or authority is very foreign and under suspect. Clearly, Satan has had an interest in keeping these things shrouded in mystery – Lest a people rise up that have an understanding of what God has ordained, and go out and destroy Satan's kingdom as they operate in these callings.

Jesus Christ has provided for a lot of things, and the Bible usually speaks in terms of the past tense to indicate just what God's intention was and still is. The Bible says that we were healed (1 Peter 2:24), that we were delivered from the power of darkness (Colossians 1:13), that we are complete (perfect) in Him (Colossians 2:10) and many other unquestionable proclamations. These are testimonials of what God has provided through the cross, which is a far cry from what we are currently enjoying or experiencing. Ignorance and disharmony with God's plan is the work of the devil to infiltrate and dismantle the foundation upon which our basic belief is built.

The king exercises authority by his edict. He rules and governs his domain under the rulership and authority of Jesus Christ, the Kings of Kings over all the earth – both natural and spiritual kings (Revelation 1:5). God does not appoint people as kings with carte blanche rule over His people. Their authority is subject to the greater ruler, Jesus the Christ. Any other command means submitting to another king – Satan. Yes, Satan also has a kingdom which is operating illegally in this world. Wherever we sin we are undoing the work of the cross in our lives by submitting once again to Satan to function through us.

Sooner or later we come to the understanding that he can only lead to death and destruction and nothing good comes from him. We were not called to be Satan's in bondage, but to be free men under God. We are called as kings to have dominion over the affairs of this world, to root out Satan's works. We are also called to be priests of the order of Melchizedek – who was not only a priest, but also a king (Hebrews 7:1).

We can attain to this prominence because of Jesus Christ, the High Priest of the Order of Melchizedek, and the King of Kings. He dwells within us and our bodies are temples unto God. Priests offer sacrifices to God, and seek to bring God and people together. Our offering is the sacrifice of praise and worship. We all have the ministry of reconciliation according to 2 Corinthians 5:18. We are all suppose to intercede before God's throne, offering praise, breaking spiritual bondages and leading men into the New Covenant.

Every believer is called to be a soul-winner, bringing forth fruits worthy of repentance. Every child of God is called to walk closely with God. Historically the people of God in the church age have been very content with the teachings of the church. This complacency has led to lethargy, we are to shake off our drowsiness and come to prayer and the spirit of God will quicken our spirit and reveal his truth to those who seek it. Complacency has led us to leave our lives in the hands of men who declare themselves as intercessors for us. The scriptures teach that there is only one intercessor between God and man and that is the Jesus Christ.

Tardiness on our behalf has led us to leave our work in the hands of a few self appointed men who claim to be men of God with special power to deliver us. It is easier to be weak and defeated than it is to exercise the kingly authority of Christ in every kind of circumstance.

The grim facts of life are not so easy. When we come to grips with the reality that we are all involved in a life and death struggle for eternal souls, attempts to strike a bargain with the enemy by sitting on the fence and playing the game of not taking sides, is futile. The words of our Lord in Matthew 12:30, "*He that is not for me is against me; and he that gather not with me scatters abroad*".

There is spiritual warfare going on and all are called to fight the good fight of faith. True repentance and true faith are required along with the physical manifestations to demonstrate the inward man. We are called to pray without ceasing, to abide in Christ and His Word. There is no class distinction of Christians. The Bible states in Matthew 18:4. "*Whosoever therefore shall humble himself as this little child, the same is greatest in the kingdom of heaven*".

"But he that is greatest among you shall be your servant." Matthew 23:11

In Jesus we are all one, conforming to His image. He came to abolish anything that would set us apart one from another. There is no longer a temple with an assigned priesthood. We are the living temple of God. It is our duty to keep it clean and sanctified by turning away from sin. We are the temple the Holy Spirit can abide in. The significance of the temple veil being torn from top to bottom was the sign of ushering in a new way of service. The ultimate sacrifice was slain; the perfect and sinless blood was shed; the price for redemption was paid; once and for all the need for sacrifice of animals was a thing of the past and man was free to come boldly to the throne of God for mercy. Jesus our High Priest now intermediates for us when we profess our weaknesses and confess our sins before God, not man.

This knowledge is not for us alone; like the cross it is to be passed both downwards to the younger generation and sideways to all our acquaintances siblings, friends and acquaintances, but they must see these values in our lives. Rebuke and correction can be done lovingly and honestly. This is a training that should be encouraged in the home. There is a tendency to soften the seriousness of the sin so the individual does not feel bad about him/herself. Circumventing the problem or watering down the seriousness of the sin is not truthful and it does not help the situation.

Children should be taught from an early age to address each other when they do something wrong. Parents should discourage tale bearing, lies and dishonesty and deal with it as soon as it happens. My wife and I insist that our children follow the rule set out in Matthew 18:15-18 in dealing with one another. If one of our children comes with a story about a sibling's wrong doing, our first question is, "Have you said anything to him or her about it?" If the answer is No, we send them back, and only if there is a disputation between them do we get involved. It is also important they understand that love is the underlying factor and not vindictiveness. This life skill will allow them to take their place in society with a clear conscience and to develop mutual respect for one another.

This onus is also on the church. Elders, deacons and ministers all have a responsibility and are accountable, one to the other. This is setting an example in the church for all to follow. Sensitivity to one's sin must also be taken into consideration but the seriousness should not be minimized to appease the individual. These are unpleasant tasks sometimes, but if the congregation understands the underlying implication and the responsibility to abide by the rules laid down in scripture then no one should feel the need to avoid addressing the problem. There will be some who will leave the congregation and feel bitter, but occasionally the olive branch should be extended by recognizing events in their lives or when they need spiritual support.

The Apostle Paul wrote in Romans chapter 6, *"we who have been joined to Christ in baptism are no longer subjected to sin. Instead, we have been given the power, through the Spirit, to wage war against the flesh and to subdue it".*

In James 3, the apostle speaks of dominion over the tongue by comparing it to the Adamic dominion over animals. This is a crucial point. Adam's fallen children continued to take dominion, building cities, discovering metallurgy, composing music increasing technological advances, building bridges that seem to defy nature. (Genesis 4), but the result of their dominion was a world filled with violence and evil. Unbelievers may have astonishing accomplishments, but outside of Christ they are slaves to sin, Satan, and death. Dominion over sin is the kind of dominion that sinners lack, and this is precisely what Christ through the Holy Spirit promises.

The area of dominion is common to both unbelievers and believers alike. Children of both unbelieving and believing parents decide how the children are to be brought up and decide on the values to be inculcated in them. The significant difference is Christian homes should instill Christian principles while in non Christian homes the ideals would be based on socially accepted ethics.

Similarly there are codes of ethics in the workplace. The book of Nehemiah displays the virtues of a believer in an ungodly environment (Matthew 20). The parable of the workers in the vineyard teaches Christian service and riches, no matter how educated a Christian is or how menial the job, he is to do the best he can to submit to the obedience of Christ rather than grumbling or complaining. Even slaves, Paul says, should work not to please men but to please Christ (Ephesians 6:5-8).

According to Exodus 17:16, the Lord declared an inter-generational war against the Amalekites because of their cruelty to Israel when they left Egypt. In like manner there is warfare in the New Covenant; the difference is this warfare is spiritual and our weapons are the Word of God (2 Corinthians 10:1-6). Our warfare is still waged, as it was in the Old Covenant, from generation to generation. By raising up a new generation of "priests and kings to God," we participate in Christ's war of conquest, looking in hope for the day when all His enemies will be placed beneath His feet (1 Corinthians 15:25).

When we think of being a king, we need to have a clear understanding of what is involved in this role. Firstly, the king must dominion over a territory. He has to have a plan to protect this territory from invasion and attack. His power is strengthened by the horses he owns, as this will influence his strategy of defense in an attack. He has to have an army of loyal, brave and courageous men. He must have guards on duty on the lookout for infiltration of the enemy. It is to his best interest that his territory expands as this is added strength. This increase is for the kingdom and not for him personally. He looks after their well being and serves them. A king must possess power and not be possessed by power. If a king does not know how to use power he could easily be overpowered by it and it can be his downfall.

Seeking the wisdom of God to rule is vital. Seeking the advice of godly men around him is also important. Listening to the voice of God and acting in obedience is what God wants; never consider your own strength above what God dictates. King Saul had thousands of soldiers, yet when he saw strong men and valiant men he took them for himself (1Sam 14:52). David on the other hand took the needy and the broken ones and gave them hope in a cause; with this common thread they gathered themselves under his leadership (1 Sam 22:2). Yet later through his success the growing pride in David's heart incited him into taking a census so the he may have grounds for boasting.

God the controller of all allowed this to be done in order to bring King David to a place of humility and reality (2 Sam 24). Both God and Satan could be involved in the same event, but for different reasons. God's rationale is so that the believer might be instructed and grow, while Satan's motive is to discredit the believer and through him to dishonour God Himself. David was chastised by God for this effrontery. This brought David to his knees in repentance. David recognized that as the king of Israel his primary task was that of a shepherd to his sheep. Despite his sins he had a tender heart and is commended as "a man after God's own heart" and he was quick to repent.

When entrusted with the role of leadership it is wise to be prayerful. Those under our authority should not be led or incited to seek worldly methods to promote our position and cause. The worldly way only leads to bondage like it did the children of Israel. The leader must not entice his followers to be beholden to the world's glories and honour; instead they should be encouraged to look only to God for wisdom and strength. This is in direct opposition to our natural instincts, faith and wisdom is the only antidote for this awesome task.

The scriptures record numerous incidents of kings acquiring many wives and concubines. Today many Christians seek out multiple partners; however Paul strongly admonishes us to refrain from such practices. Looking back at the Old Testament where even holy men and prophets were engaged in having multiple wives we see the corresponding disunity in the home causing them much grief.

David our hero is a prime example, Absalom his son, murdered his brother, rebelled against his father and even contended for his throne. His ultimate death broke David's heart. Solomon's quest to strengthen his kingdom set him on a mission of making alliances with other nations through marriage. The disparity in culture and spirituality of his wives was his downfall yet he was the world's wisest man. This is a telling tale of the wisdom of this world compared to God's wisdom. It is also a clear indication that even though God did not condemn polygamy in the Old Testament such marriages brought much disunity in the family. We see the heartache of Leah and Rachael, two sisters fighting for the affection of one man. We are still reaping the discord of Abraham's attempt to fulfill God's promise as guided by his wife Sarah rather than the one who gave him the promise.

One of Satan's victories in causing dissension is his endeavour to foil God's plans. The multiple wives acquired by men of old were God's submissive will not His perfect will. The heathen wives taken by Solomon and Sampson were against God's commandment. Paul in the New Testament was very direct in admonishing believers against this practice.

The world seeks power through wealth and being able to win the favours of others. There is a basic need in all of us to accumulate wealth in some form or another. For some it is gives a sense of security, for many it is a basic necessity for survival, but there are those who regard it as power. Women, like money, fill the same need. There are men who use money to satisfy their lust after a woman who under natural circumstances would be unattainable by him but wealth will place him in the class where he is able to interact socially and eventually achieve his goal. God has created human beings with these instincts but it is only when greed is applied to the equation that the scene becomes ugly. Man's carnal nature will cause him to lose his soul.

Envy and greed leads to seduction and murder. The truth is that all God wants man to know is how to exercise balance in all things. This is not a male problem as both men and women are guilty in these passions although it is more prevalent among men. Each sex may go about accomplishing their goals differently but the underlying causes are basically the same. When man can come to grips with his natural limitations and look to God for guidance then he does not live a life of conflict. Instead peace and contentment are the fruits to be enjoyed. While the glitter offered by the world can leave a man empty as he seeks to conquer greater things only to bring to fruition death and destruction.

Man craving should be a thirst after truth and truth can only be found in the person of Christ Himself (Jn 14:6), and the full truth is the fullness of Christ. The law of the Old Testament and grace of the New Testament are Christ revealed. In the Old Testament He is veiled while in the New He is revealed; the mystery that was coded through all ages. We as children of God are to walk in the fullness of all that is revealed to us, and live by every word known to us (Matt 4:4) without compromising (V20), and at the same time be complete in the new depths and new revelations of truth that God will continually unfold to us.

THE VISION

I HAD A vision of being in a service; there was a sense of God's power in our midst then during the worship I was transported into another realm. Suddenly I felt the compelling presence of the Holy Spirit became very dominant and I was being directed to the altar. I reverenced the altar and I would not dare approach it without just cause. I fear God too much to trivialize the altar, yet the prominence of the Holy Spirit could not be ignored. The consciousness of my sinful nature made me react with deep humility while my faith in God opened a doorway to my inner man and I was received without any distractions. There were about 400 other people in the crowd, and as the worship service continued there was a spiritual restoration taking place simultaneously with the service. Words are inadequate to express what was transpiring and it would be futile to even try to illustrate such an awe inspiring sensation.

It was at a point in my life that I was seeking direction from God as to the purpose of my life. There was a deep cry within me to refocus as to what I was being called to do. I was torn between my present pastoral duties and my previous evangelistic involvement. While I was before the altar, I prostrated myself on the floor as the intensity of the power of God increased. I was cognizant of His glory; then supernaturally I was moved to another level. I beheld an inexhaustible crowd mostly in wheel chairs. They were able to extricate themselves and walked towards the altar. This caused a commotion in the auditorium and attracted the attention of the reporters, the media and onlookers.

Ambulances, buses and cars were filled to capacity waiting with people from all nationalities and age groups, in various deficient health conditions, twisted, fragile and frail; their conditions seemed hopeless. There was a line up of the medical team identifying the various maladies before them. In their ill state they were worshipping God. A cloud of Glory was formed over the platform where the people were as a result of this worship. The cloud grew larger and denser as the devotion continued and as they caught a glimpse of the cloud they were being restored to health in a dynamic way pulsating with energy. Through this surge of energy the assembly responded with a resounding praise of love and unity. Suddenly the glory that had formed like a rain cloud, rather than descend as one would expect, started to change colours instead.

This new development, caused by the upsurge of praise, continued as the worshippers persisted in their praise; the entire building was enveloped in a cloud. The resultant effect was that everyone present: – young and old, skeptics and believers, church and unchurched experienced a physical change. Their faces glowed and as this glow transmitted among those gathered, they grew delirious with emotions of every kind. There were demonstrations of crying, laughing, prostrating and hands raised in praise and worship. Some seemed caught up with what was happening and were mystified by the effect of the Holy Spirit. They were mesmerized by the open display of emotions, but there were some who gave their service to help those whom they felt were out of control and needed their help to keep order so that the work of the Holy Spirit would not be disrupted. Many were crying in unison "He is holy, He is holy". Their voices were in an undulating unity, the rise and fall of their voices brought to mind the rush and lull of the waves of the sea. During the lull a warm heat was generated which brought the healing and miracles.

As the healing continued many of the unchurched were weeping, penitently confessing their remorse of their disobedience, while some remained speechless. A remorseful and apologetic group at the altar resigned themselves into His care. There in the distance were sounds of rejoicing and celebration, the presence of the Holy Spirit was having a bleaching effect on all as they were being cleansed of their sins. It was a supernatural phenomena and an incredible life altering experience.

The ambiance was like an early Christmas morning. A joyous mood filled everyone like a large family, each filled with expectation. Just before I woke up, I saw like an image in a photo of me standing on the platform looking out into the crowd below.

This vision I had was at a meeting held on a Friday service at the church I attended. The following Sunday morning after worship, I went to the bookstore of the church, and to my amazement, I saw the identical photo on the cover of a book. I was dumbfounded at this experience. I am aware that God is able to do things that defy the imagination, and these occurrences are individual and rare. Yet I did not know how to interpret it. I was filled with mixed emotions for there was an air of greater responsibility, and my prayers were being answered. The person on the cover of the book was Kathryn Kuhlman on the platform of a crusade looking into the crowd, the same crowd I saw. Through a friend I learnt about Kathryn Kuhlman many years before, however we were never interested in her ministry because we were given the wrong impression of her and her ministry.

Never before had I witnessed a healing ministry and her ministry was extraordinary. All I could remember was her voice which sounded ghostly and theatrical. Apparently there was great excitement as healings took place but, the video did not capture the excitement. The angle of the camera did not give much of a view as to what was really happening. I became curious in her and her ministry. I set about reading her story, and listened to her teaching. There was a hunger to learn from her ministry, I could not get my mind off the vision of her in the snapshot. I needed answers to so many questions. Something about her resonated in me, she had what I was looking for. It seems someone was directing me as to the path I am to take and she was the model of that path.

It was through her ministry that I became acquainted with Benny Hinn's meetings. Here is another person who the Lord had put in my path to confirm and affirm the glimpse he revealed to me many years ago. When we consider the men and women who had a glimpse of the glory of God, we see how transformed their lives are because they are infected with His holiness and it is against the grain of their morals to revert to the ways of the world. With holiness comes the resurrection power of Christ. The Holy Spirit is here to administer this power to us. We cannot begin to imagine His capabilities, we are limited in our thinking and He has no boundaries, therefore all we can do is to submit and surrender. When He is in control then and only then we become recipients of His Glory, then we catch that glimpse that is priceless.

In God's presence it is difficult to anticipate how to conduct ourselves. The flesh will always want to be in control, it is our nature and it is difficult to act outside the flesh. Only seasoned individuals are able to surrender to the voice of the Holy Spirit. Not knowing how to react can be disruptive because our focus can be on self and those around us are influencing our reaction. It is only when in our total surrender that we yield because flesh has no part in this. The power that is now released allows us full capitulation and nothing else matters, because the flesh has been defeated. The experience of the peace and joy that is exhumed is exhilarating, and with His power it captivates the spirit into oneness with God.

> *"Living creatures cry out day and night "Holy, holy, holy, is the Lord God Almighty".* Revelations 4:8-10

This is a picture of the angels of the Lord conducting themselves in His presence by crying out Holy! Holy! Holy! We see the twenty four elders prostrating in pure worship before God who sits on the throne who never get tired of bowing because their bowing is in response of their continual amazement of being captivated, enthralled and spellbound. They are so captivated that no sooner they get up they are down on their knees again. (Rev 11:16). He is given honour by having faces to the ground to show Him reverence. He is worthy of this honour and anything less would dishonour Him. (Rev 7:11).

Moses was required to take off his shoes as a sign of respect of His Holiness. (Exodus 3:5). We have to come to the understanding of this awesome God that we serve that we should give Him the most utmost respect due Him. Nothing else should matter other than to fulfil our purpose to love and worship Him with humility and a contrite heart. It is priceless and something that His children not take for granted.

My desire is that we all come to the place of true worship and reverence for our God. To see Him for who He truly is. To have a desire to be in His presence daily, seeking His face and honouring Him. Allowing the Holy Spirit to be our coach and us to be His athlete will enhance our walk as a believer and bring us closer to the reality of God. We will experience true power and strength as we see the reality of God unveil before our eyes. I pray that many will experience the awesome presence of the Holy Spirit, and desire to know Him as a real person. To walk hand in hand with Him and explore all that He has to offer to those who love the Lord. He is not just the third person of the trinity, but a person in a spirit form. Developing a relationship takes time and effort, just like a marriage, and if we persevere in this venture we can truly make a difference in the world around us.

For more information or other books, contact:
Harrison Mungal
P.O. Box 30225, Toronto, ON
M9W 1P0. Canada.

Receive two years free tuition at Metro Bible College with the purchase of this book. Call 416-523-7602, email: *info@metrobiblecollege.ca*, visit our web page at *www.metrobiblecollege.ca* or write to Metro Bible College, P.O. Box 30225, Toronto, On. M9W 1P0. Canada. Quote reference # HSMC08

relying on the Holy Spirit to be our coach